The Little Bighorn campaign 1876

Sioux Warrior versus US Cavalryman

COMBAT

Ron Field

Illustrated by Adam Hook

OSPREY PUBLISHING
Bloomsbury Publishing Plc
PO Box 883, Oxford, OX1 9PL, UK
1385 Broadway, 5th Floor, New York, NY 10018, USA
E-mail: info@ospreypublishing.com
www.ospreypublishing.com

OSPREY is a trademark of Osprey Publishing Ltd

First published in Great Britain in 2019

© Osprey Publishing Ltd, 2019

All rights reserved. No part of this publication may be reproduced or transmitted in any form or by any means, electronic or mechanical, including photocopying, recording, or any information storage or retrieval system, without prior permission in writing from the publishers.

A catalog record for this book is available from the British Library.

ISBN: PB 9781472831880; eBook 9781472832214;
ePDF 9781472832207; XML 9781472832191

19 20 21 22 23   10 9 8 7 6 5 4 3 2 1

Maps by www.bounford.com
Index by Rob Munro
Typeset by PDQ Digital Media Solutions, Bungay, UK
Printed in China through World Print Ltd.

Osprey Publishing supports the Woodland Trust, the UK's leading woodland conservation charity.

To find out more about our authors and books visit www.ospreypublishing.com. Here you will find extracts, author interviews, details of forthcoming events and the option to sign up for our newsletter.

Acknowledgments

I am greatly indebted to Frederic C. Wagner III for sharing his limitless knowledge of the battle at the Little Bighorn. Thanks also to Dori Wagner-Eldridge; Cindy Hagen, Cultural Resource Manager, Little Bighorn Battlefield National Monument, MT; Daisy Njoku, Anthropology Archives, Smithsonian Museum Support Center, MD; Marlana Cook, Curator of Art, West Point Museum, NY; Coi E. Drummond-Gehrig, Denver Public Library Western Collection; Renee Harvey, Librarian, Helmerich Center for American Research at Gilcrease Museum, Tulsa, OK; Dale Kosman; and John Langellier.

Artist's note

Readers may care to note that the original paintings from which the color plates in this book were prepared are available for private sale. All reproduction copyright whatsoever is retained by the publishers. All inquiries should be addressed to:

Scorpio, 158 Mill Road, Hailsham, East Sussex BN27 2SH, UK
Email: scorpiopaintings@btinternet.com

The publishers regret that they can enter into no correspondence upon this matter.

CONTENTS

INTRODUCTION	4
THE OPPOSING SIDES	8
Recruitment, training, and organization • Appearance, weapons, and equipment • Conduct in battle	
THE ROSEBUD	23
June 17, 1876	
THE LITTLE BIGHORN	36
June 25, 1876	
SLIM BUTTES	57
September 9–10, 1876	
ANALYSIS	70
The Rosebud • The Little Bighorn • Slim Buttes	
AFTERMATH	74
ORDERS OF BATTLE	76
SELECT BIBLIOGRAPHY	78
INDEX	80

Introduction

OPPOSITE
In 1874, the US government disregarded their treaty with the Sioux and dispatched a military and civilian expedition led by Lt. Col. George A. Custer to look for a suitable location for a military fort in the Black Hills and to find a route from the Northern Missouri River to the southwest. Produced by British photographer William H. Illingworth, this view shows the head of Custer's expedition into the Black Hills which confirmed the discovery of gold and was a major cause of the Great Sioux War. (US National Archives NWDNS-77-HQ-264-854)

Gun smoke and dust rose above the bluffs by the camp in the Greasy Grass Valley as the warriors led by Crazy Horse closed in on the US Army soldiers who had dared to attack them. War whoops rent the air as the Sioux and Cheyenne frantically whipped their ponies toward the cavalrymen huddled on what was to become known as "Last Stand Hill." According to the Cheyenne chief Two Moons, "Some of the soldiers were down on their knees, some standing. Officers all in front. The smoke was like a great cloud, and everywhere the Sioux went the dust rose like smoke. We circled all round – swirling like water round a stone. We shoot, we ride fast, we shoot again. Soldiers drop, and horses fall on them …" (Garland 1898: 446). It was all over during the next few minutes and Lt. Col. George A. Custer and 209 men of the 7th Cavalry, including scouts and civilians, lay dead.

The events which led to one of the greatest disasters in American military history gathered momentum in 1868, when the Fort Laramie Treaty set aside a portion of the Lakota lands as the Great Sioux Reservation. This comprised the western half of Dakota Territory, including the Black Hills, for the exclusive use of the Native American. It also recognized as Lakota Sioux, Northern Cheyenne, and Arapaho hunting grounds a large "unceded territory" in Wyoming and Montana territories, plus the Powder River Country. In all these areas, non-Native Americans were forbidden to trespass, except for officials of the US government.

Unfortunately, settlers continued to encroach on Dakota Territory and by 1872 government officials were considering harvesting the rich timber resources of the Black Hills to provide lumber for the construction of new settlements. In 1871 a commission approached the Red Cloud Agency, established on the North Platte River in Wyoming Territory, about the possibility of their signing away the Black Hills for $6 million, but the Lakota Sioux refused the offer.

ABOVE Entitled "The Custer Fight," this painting produced by Charles M. Russell depicts Sioux and Cheyenne warriors closing in around the remains of Custer's battalion on "Last Stand Hill." (Library of Congress LC-USZC4-7160)

In May 1875, Sioux delegations headed by Red Cloud, Spotted Tail, and Lone Horn traveled to Washington, DC in a last-ditch attempt to persuade President Ulysses S. Grant to honor the existing treaty terms and stop the flow of miners on to their lands. They were bluntly informed that Congress wanted to pay their tribes $25,000 for the land and have them relocated to Indian Territory, which is present-day Oklahoma. The delegates refused to sign a new treaty and returned home.

During the fall of 1875, a US commission visited the Indian agencies to persuade the Lakota people to bring pressure on their leaders to sign the new treaty, but failed. Meanwhile, the Black Hills became the center of a growing crisis as thousands of Sioux and Cheyenne led by Sitting Bull and Crazy Horse

The Great Sioux War

MAP KEY

The battles explored in this book took place in the United States frontier territories of Montana and Dakota. Following the refusal of Sioux leaders Sitting Bull and Crazy Horse to lead their people into reservations to make way for logging and gold prospecting, the US Army ordered Lt. Gen. Philip H. Sheridan, commander of the Military Division of the Missouri, to march three military columns into the area to defeat the Native Americans. Commanding the District of Montana, Col. John Gibbon marched south and then east from Fort Shaw. Commanding the Department of Dakota, Brig. Gen. Alfred H. Terry led a column west from Fort Abraham Lincoln on the Missouri River. Commanding the Department of the Platte, Brig. Gen. George R. Crook progressed north from Fort Fetterman in Wyoming Territory. On June 17, Crook's column was fought to a standstill in the Rosebud Valley by about 1,000 Sioux and Cheyenne warriors led by Crazy Horse, and prevented from locating the main Sioux encampment. Five days later, Lt. Col. George A. Custer, commanding the 7th Cavalry, marched out from Terry's column and advanced toward the valley of the Little Bighorn where, on June 25, the battalion led by Maj. Marcus A. Reno failed to press home their attack on the southern end of a vast Sioux encampment, and Custer's battalion, amounting to 268 men, was soon after annihilated farther north on "Last Stand Hill." On September 9, an advanced battalion of Crook's column, led by Capt. Anson Mills, 5th Cavalry, attacked and captured the village of American Horse and retrieved Native American trophies taken at the Little Bighorn.

refused to come into the Indian agencies for council by January 31, 1876. On March 10, Indian agent Dexter E. Clapp, of the Crow Agency in Montana, advised John Q. Smith, Commissioner of Indian Affairs, that the Sioux were occupying part of the Crow Reservation, and by their constant warfare were paralyzing all efforts to induce the Mountain Crows to undertake agriculture or other means of self-support. On February 8, 1876, the Army was ordered to treat all Native Americans outside the Indian agencies as opponents, and preparations for a winter military campaign against the Sioux and their allies were begun.

Civilian miners accompanying Custer's expedition discovered gold on French Creek on August 1, 1874, and Custer sent a dispatch to Fort Laramie confirming the find. A gold rush ensued as prospectors flooded into the Black Hills in violation of the Fort Laramie Treaty. Created from a photograph by Stanley J. Morrow, this engraving was published in *Frank Leslie's Illustrated Newspaper* on March 25, 1876, and shows a gold-prospecting expedition of 247 wagons leaving Yankton, Dakota Territory, for the Black Hills. (Author's collection)

MONTANA TERRITORY
DAKOTA TERRITORY
WYOMING TERRITORY
IDAHO TERRITORY
NEBRASKA
Fort Benton
Fort Shaw
Fort Ellis
Fort Peck
Fort Buford
Fort Totten
DEVILS LAKE RESERVATION
Fort Abraham Lincoln
Fort F.D. Pease
Fort C.F. Smith (abandoned)
Fort Phil Kearny (abandoned)
Fort Fetterman
Fort Laramie
Fort Randall
SIOUX–ASSINIBOINE RESERVATION
ARICKAREE, MANDAN & GROS VENTRE RESERVATION
CROW RESERVATION
GREAT SIOUX RESERVATION
Crow Agency
Camp Supply
Glendive Depot
Powder River Depot
Standing Rock Agency
Cheyenne River Agency
Crow Creek Agency
Lower Brule Agency
Spotted Tail Agency
Red Cloud Agency
GIBBON
TERRY
CUSTER
Terry
CROOK
SIOUX & CHEYENNE
Sitting Bull & Crazy Horse
Crazy Horse
SLIM BUTTES
Crook City
Deadwood
BLACK HILLS
ROCKY MOUNTAINS
BIGHORN MOUNTAINS
Sun River
Missouri River
Mussel Shell River
Yellowstone River
Tullock Creek
Little Bighorn River
Bighorn River
Rosebud Creek
Tongue River
Goose Creek
Prairie Dog Creek
Mizpah Creek
Powder River
Little Powder River
Glendive Creek
Beaver Creek
Little Missouri River
Heart River
Cannonball River
Grand River
Moreau River
Gap Creek
Belle Fourche River
Cheyenne River
White River
Niobrara River
North Platte River
Sheyenne River
James River
Forts
Camps and depots
Indian Agencies
Reservations
N
0
50 miles
0
50km

The Opposing Sides

RECRUITMENT, TRAINING, AND ORGANIZATION

Sioux

Warfare was a way of life for the Sioux. Training for battle began at a very young age for Sioux boys. They were taught to handle bows and arrows, and played arduous games of the roughest character which simulated the demands of the battlefield. On reaching adolescence, boys often accompanied war parties, serving as water carriers.

Essential to battle training for the Sioux were the various warrior societies which taught fighting skills to young men and developed a warrior ethos. Members of these societies would form war or hunting parties, but when their tribe went into battle society members did not fight as coordinated units. Members of the Crow Owner Society were experienced and proven warriors who emulated the crow, in that they strove to be first in battle to strike the enemy, as the crow was first to fall upon dead warriors on the field. Arrows fired by these warriors were believed to fly as straight as the crow, and the warriors often rode into battle with stuffed crows draped around their necks. Warriors of the Kit Fox Society were expected to pledge bravery, generosity, and honor in war, and were renowned for concern and good acts within the tribe in peacetime. Members of the Strong Heart Society pledged self-control in their thoughts and actions, and cared for the poor and needy, while the Badger Society was pledged to take on the aspect of the fearless badger. The White Marked Society was composed of hardened veterans. Often comprised of younger warriors, the Bare Lance Owners Society was symbolic of those waiting to collect war honors in battle. Warriors of the Mandan Society, also called the "owl headdress society," pledged to sacrifice their lives, if need be, to save a wounded comrade.

Sioux chief Crow King wears the coat of a US Army major. Crow King was involved in the fighting with Crazy Horse in Deep Coulee and on Calhoun Hill, and provided important eyewitness accounts of the battle of the Little Bighorn in later years. (US National Archives 111-SC-82525)

Although organized units did not exist in the Native American way of fighting, they may have employed methods to rally and regroup their warriors. At the Little Bighorn, Army scout George Herendeen observed, "five chiefs, and each one carried a flag for their men to rally around. Some of the flags were red, others yellow, white and blue, and one a black flag" (*ANJ*, July 15, 1876: 792). The red banner that Herendeen witnessed on this occasion may have belonged to Crazy Horse, as he carried a similar marker during the Powder River campaign of 1865 (Bray 2006: 88).

COMBAT Sioux warrior

This plate depicts a Sioux warrior charging toward the column of Brig. Gen. George R. Crook in the Rosebud Valley. With his lance leveled, the warrior echoes the Sioux war cry "Hokahe – Hokahe [Let's go]." This figure is based on the warrior Lazy White Bull, a nephew of Sitting Bull, who recalled that the battle at the Rosebud was one of the fiercest fights he ever saw.

The Rosebud, Montana Territory, June 17, 1876

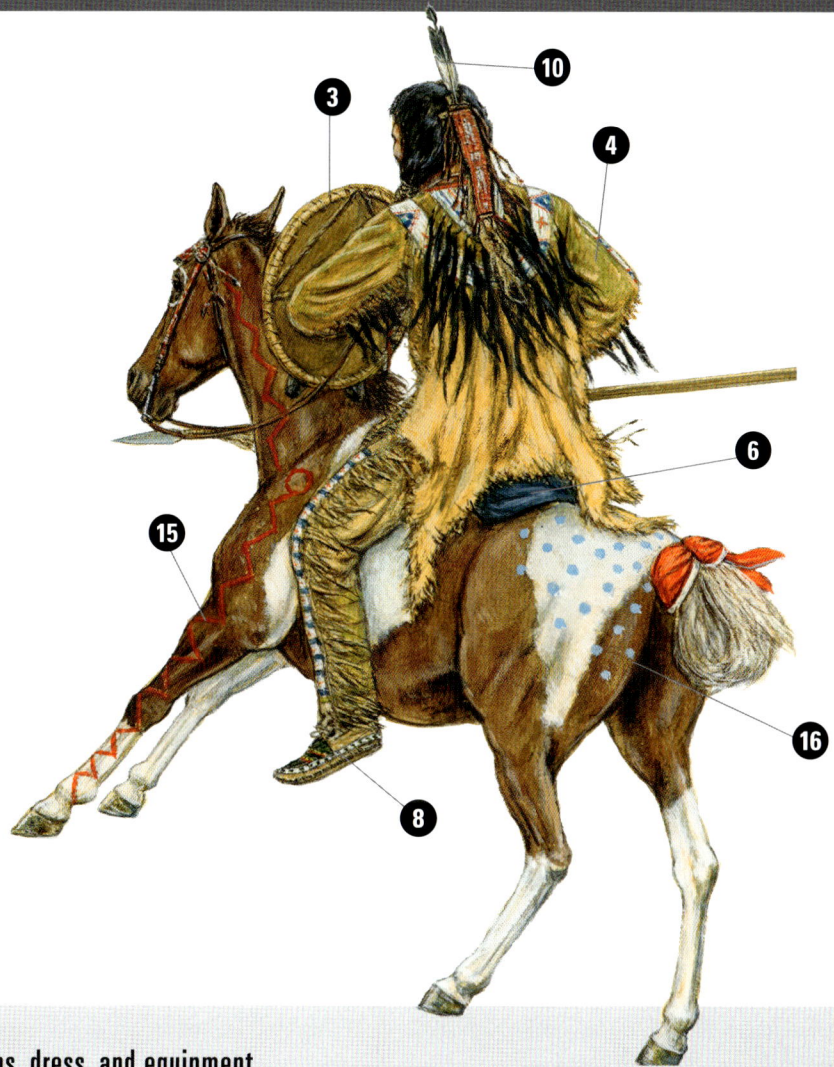

Weapons, dress, and equipment

His main weapon is a lance (**1**) 6ft in length, tipped with a 12in, hand-forged blade and decorated with feathers and a rawhide fringe of 24 strands, consisting of a multiple of four, donating the power of the wind to drive the lance to its mark. He has tied around his waist by a narrow leather strap a knife (**2**) with bone handle and hide sheath with quill decoration and copper and cloth fringe and strands. Important for its spiritual protection as well as for physical defense, his war shield (**3**) is composed of buffalo rawhide covered with buckskin and painted with his personal, and vision-related, design incorporating a "thunderbird" which he believed represented a good spirit, guardian of truth, and protector of men.

He wears a war shirt (**4**) made of deerskin which he believed had intrinsic spiritual powers which were transferred to him. Its top half and arms are painted greasy olive green; blue, white, and red beadwork strips are attached to the chest and arms. The neck has a red band and beadwork bib at front and back. The locks of hair attached to his shirt represent the people of the tribe for whom he is responsible. A hair pipe breastplate (**5**) protects his chest. He also has a blue calico breechclout (**6**), and fringed buckskin leggings (**7**) with blue, white, and red beaded strips, greasy green and black paintwork below the knee, and long fringes mixed with more locks of hair. His deerskin moccasins (**8**) have a beaded cross decoration consisting of turquoise, powder blue, greasy yellow, and red on a white background. Signifying the free flow of life, his long hair (**9**) is braided at the front. Indicating he has counted coup, he wears a single eagle feather (**10**) attached to the back of his head by a leather cross patch. He has painted a yellow line (**11**) across his forehead to indicate a thunderstorm on the horizon.

The warrior rides a piebald pony bareback with a red and white beaded and quilled horsehide headstall (**12**), and tail tied up for war with a wide strip (**13**) of red trade cloth with white selvage, or stitched, edge. The pony is painted with a white circle (**14**) around its eyes for keener eyesight and red lightning bolts (**15**) down its neck and onto its forelegs to incorporate speed and agility. The blue roundels (**16**) on its rump indicate the number of encampments its rider has raided. Assuming the warrior weighs about 145lb, his pony is carrying only about 155lb into combat.

US cavalry

All enlisted men of the US cavalry of 1876 were volunteers aged from 18 to 35. The average age of recruits was 23 for first enlistments, and 32 for those who re-enlisted. Few of these men were educated and many were illiterate. Financial hardship, industrial strikes, and general economic upheaval produced many native-born recruits for whom the Army offered a viable means of earning a living. Many recruits were recent immigrants, arriving chiefly from Ireland, Germany, or England, with Canada, Scotland, France, and Switzerland furnishing most of the others. Many of the immigrant recruits had seen service in European armies. Some had campaigned with British forces in India and Africa, while others had fought in conflicts such as the Franco-Prussian War of 1870–71. The total number of European and other foreign-born men represented 42.9 percent of the enlisted personnel of the 7th Cavalry. Enlistment in the US Army would have offered a familiar haven for these men upon arrival in a strange country.

The principal recruiting stations were at St. Louis, Chicago, Indianapolis, Buffalo, Pittsburgh, Boston, and New York. Branch offices were opened in several more western cities to secure recruits needed following the Custer massacre. Many recruits were also signed up by roving recruiting details sent out by individual regiments.

Army service was not generally viewed as a popular career option by many and most regiments were under strength. During the 1876 campaign, the 7th Cavalry was operating at only 60 percent strength, with companies containing only from 40 to 60 men each. Prior to the Little Bighorn disaster, cavalry recruits were required to be at least 5ft 5in tall and weigh not more than 155lb. During the weeks following the disaster, 2,500 recruits were called for. As a result, the height requirement was reduced to 5ft 3in and maximum weight increased to 175lb. Enlisted men were paid $13 a month. Following congressional action to increase the size of the cavalry branch of service on August 15, 1876, the official company limit was raised from 70 to 100 men, and many of those recruited to fill the expanded companies were popularly called "Custer's Avengers."

All cavalry recruits were sent to Jefferson Barracks in St. Louis, Missouri where, upon arrival, they were assigned to a recruit troop of instruction. Re-enlisted soldiers were often appointed temporary sergeants and corporals to instruct new recruits. Enlisting underage

Built on the west bank of the Missouri River in Dakota Territory in 1872, Fort Abraham Lincoln was home to the 7th Cavalry for three years prior to the battle of the Little Bighorn. This panoramic view was produced c.1875. (Little Bighorn Battlefield National Monument LIBI_00019_00214)

in Cincinnati, Ohio, during September 1875, William C. Slaper was assigned to Co. M, 7th Cavalry, and wrote: "A few days later, twenty of us recruits were sent to Jefferson Barracks, St. Louis. Here we remained about six weeks, where we were instructed in the dismounted drill, and given some preliminary training at stables. We were taught how to groom a horse in regulation style, by a crusty old sergeant named "Bully" Welch, a character whom old cavalrymen of that day will remember" (*HT*, November 2, 1923: 5:1).

Some contemporary sources claimed that the ranks of the cavalry regiments involved in the 1876 campaign contained new recruits who were untested and improperly trained. Indeed, a correspondent in the *Army & Navy Journal* commented on "the raw condition of the cavalry recruits in Terry's column" during June/July 1876 (*ANJ*, August 26, 1876: 38). However, an examination of the length of service of troopers of the 7th Cavalry at the Little Bighorn reveals that, of 576 men present at the battle, 471 had served over one year, 201 had served over six months, and only nine men had less than six months' experience in the saddle (Wagner 2016: 212.)

A cavalry regiment was commanded by a colonel, lieutenant colonel, and three majors, and consisted of 12 companies. A cavalry company was authorized three officers and 70 enlisted men, and was commanded by a captain, first lieutenant, or second lieutenant, dependent on availability of rank. Following the Little Bighorn massacre this was raised to 100 men to aid in fighting the Native Americans. Company officers were assisted by a first sergeant, quartermaster sergeant, and commissary sergeant. In theory, a company also contained five sergeants, four corporals, two musicians, a wagoner, two farriers/blacksmiths, and a saddler. In reality, company strength varied dependent on availability of men. For example, the fullest company of the 7th Cavalry at the Little Bighorn (Co. L) contained two officers and 57 men, while the smallest company (Co. K) had two officers and only 41 men (Wagner 2016: 212–13).

George A. Custer and his wife Libby were photographed by Orlando Scott Goff in their study in Fort Abraham Lincoln, Dakota Territory, in 1873. Note the gun rack at far right which includes several .45-caliber Navy Colts plus the .442-caliber First Model Webley Royal Irish Constabulary revolver Custer is believed to have carried at the Little Bighorn. A large framed map of the United States and its territories leans against the wall behind Custer, while cased binoculars and his undress cap hang from a rack at far left. (Little Bighorn Battlefield National Monument LIBI 00019 00219)

COMBAT
Sergeant, Co. D, 3d Cavalry

This plate depicts a non-commissioned officer of Co. D, 3d Cavalry, during a mounted charge led by Lt. Col. William B. Royall along Kollmar Creek in the early stages of the fight at the Rosebud. The figure is based on Irish-born 29-year-old 1/Sgt. Joseph Robinson, who was one of four men of the 3d Cavalry to be awarded the Congressional Medal of Honor for gallantry in action on June 17, 1876.

The Rosebud, Montana Territory, June 17, 1876

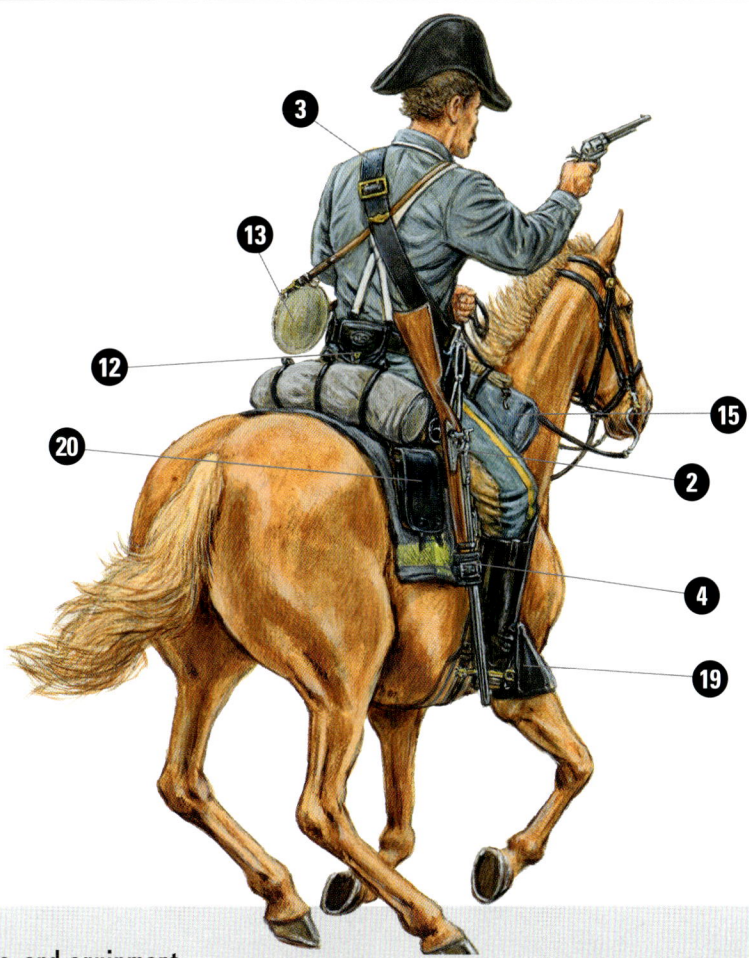

Weapons, dress, and equipment

The trooper grasps a .45-caliber Model 1873 Colt six shot, single-action revolver (**1**), with 7½in barrel; maximum effective range was approximately 100yd, although accuracy was radically reduced while in motion on horseback. When not in use this revolver was carried in an 1875-pattern holster. He is also armed with a .45-70 Model 1873 Springfield single-shot carbine (**2**); usually reserved for dismounted skirmish formation, this weapon has a 1,000yd maximum range and a 250yd effective range. It is suspended on his right side, attached via a sliding ring and bar on its butt to a swiveling snap hook on a broad leather sling (**3**) worn over his left shoulder. Its barrel is thrust into a bridle leather socket (**4**) buckled to the rear offside "D" ring of the saddle quarter strap.

The broad brim of his 1872-pattern campaign hat (**5**) has been hooked up either side. His 1874-pattern flannel pullover shirt (**6**) has white trim around the collar and placket front. A bandana (**7**) is knotted under his collar. The seat and inside leg of his regulation 1872-pattern kersey trousers are reinforced with buckskin, and have 1in-wide yellow seam stripes (**8**) denoting his rank. He also wears canvas suspenders with leather loops (**9**), and 14in-tall 1872-pattern boots (**10**) over which are cast-brass spurs with black leather straps.

At the front of his 1874-pattern black leather saber belt, with brass plate, he has two 1874-pattern cartridge slides (**11**), each capable of carrying 20 carbine cartridges. Another 22 rounds are carried in the Dyer carbine cartridge pouch (**12**) on the back of his belt. His 1874-pattern pistol cartridge pouch (not visible) contains only 12 rounds for his revolver. An 1871-pattern canteen (**13**) with wool cover is suspended over his right shoulder from a leather strap. An extra canteen is attached to his saddle (**14**).

He sits a black leather-covered Model 1872 saddle, with brass fittings. He has a rolled 1874-pattern blouse (**15**) secured by six leather straps in front of the pommel. His blanket roll, overcoat, with spare clothing rolled inside, and lariat and picket pin are strapped on top (**16**). The rest of his horse equipment consists of a six-buckle black leather bridle, separate halter, and reins (**17**); Model 1872 curb bit (**18**); pommel pouches, horse brush (near side), and shoe and nail (off side); wooden stirrups (**19**) with leather hood; linen webbing saddle girth; and Model 1874 leather saddle bags (**20**). Cavalry horses could also carry a forage sack containing about 12lb of oats strapped on the cantle of the saddle, and an 1874-pattern cotton duck haversack. Assuming the trooper weighs about 150lb, his horse is carrying roughly 230lb into combat.

APPEARANCE, WEAPONS, AND EQUIPMENT

Sioux

Each warrior society had its own distinctive appearance. Warriors of the Kit Fox Society wore a fox skin around the shoulders with the head hanging down in front and the tail down their back. Warriors of the Strong Heart Society often wore a feather headdress with buffalo horns on the sides. Members of the Badger Society carried crooked lances wrapped in wolfskin and wore otter fur around their wrists and neck. They are also believed to have embedded mirrors in the otter fur to reflect the sun and blind the enemy in battle. The veterans of the White Marked Society wore feathered headdresses which trailed to the ground, and collected white eagle feathers with black tips as battle honors. Each warrior of the Mandan Society wore a long sash which he would stake into the ground, thereby pinning himself so he could not retreat in a desperate battle. He would fight to the death, and would only move from the spot if a fellow Mandan member released the stake.

In describing the appearance of the Sioux at the Rosebud on June 17, 1876, Capt. Azor H. Nickerson, one of Brig. Gen. George R. Crook's *aides-de-camp*, confirmed the involvement of warriors of the White Marked and Strong Heart societies, by observing that many "wore the long Sioux war bonnet of eagle's plumes, which floated and fluttered in the air, back of the wearer, to the distance of five or six feet; while others wore half masks of the heads of wild animals with the ears and sometimes the horns, still protruding, giving them the appearance of devils from the nether world …" (Crook-Kennon Papers 1876).

Based on a sketch by Charles St. G. Stanley, this fanciful engraving was published in *Frank Leslie's Illustrated Newspaper* on August 12, 1876, and depicts the Sioux charging toward Lt. Col. William B. Royall's battalion at the Rosebud on June 17, 1876. (Library of Congress LC-USZ62-54652)

Based on archeological evidence in the form of shell casings found at the Little Bighorn site, the Sioux and Cheyenne were well armed with no fewer than 300 repeating rifles which included Model 1873 Winchesters and Model 1860 Spencers. Revolvers included Model 1872 Colts and New Model Army Remingtons. Eyewitness accounts of action at the Rosebud and Slim Buttes indicates continued use of this weaponry. According to a report in the *Army & Navy Journal* on August 26, 1876, ammunition for these firearms was sold by unscrupulous dealers at the Standing Rock and Brule Indian agencies.

US cavalry

Full dress, which included an 1872-pattern helmet with yellow horsehair plume and yellow-trimmed coat, was not worn on campaign by the US cavalryman of 1876, and would not have immediately been issued to the new recruits raised following the Little Bighorn massacre. Preparing to campaign with Crook at the beginning of 1876, 1/Lt. Charles King, of Co. K, 5th Cavalry, recalled that "the men stowed away their helmets and full-dress uniforms, their handsome belts and equipments, and lovingly reproduced the old Arizona slouch hats and 'thimble belts'" (King 1890: 8).

The basic issue service uniform for enlisted men consisted of an 1872-pattern dark blue flannel blouse, or sack coat, with a single row of five brass "eagle" buttons and yellow trim on collar and cuffs, although some men may have worn an 1872-pattern plaited fatigue blouse with nine-button front and yellow-trimmed collar, yoke, and cuffs, or Civil War surplus four-button sack coats. Non-commissioned officers were distinguished by yellow chevrons. Trousers were plain sky-blue kersey with reinforced seat and inner leg for saddle wear. Sergeants wore a 1in yellow stripe on the outer seam, while that for corporals was ½in wide. Pattern-1872 coarse pullover shirts were gray flannel or knit, although some men received dark-blue shirts issued on an experimental basis. Forage caps were of plain blue cloth with "crossed sabers" insignia and company letter at the front. Footwear consisted of brogans and 1872-issue knee-high boots with brass-screwed soles.

On campaign, the seasoned cavalryman wore a great variety of non-regulation clothing and headgear. In particular, officers preferred to wear enlisted men's uniforms as they were less distinguishable to an enemy. A report in the *Army & Navy Journal* during August 1876 commented: "Both the officers and men set the regulations at naught, and dress very much as their fancy or their purses direct. Some are content with the regulation pants and blue shirt; others, more stylish, afford white corduroy breeches and tall riding boots, with any kind of shirts" (*ANJ*, August 19, 1876: 22). Commanding Co. K, 7th Cavalry at the Little Bighorn, 1/Lt. Edward S. Godfrey recalled that nearly all the men had their trousers reinforced with white canvas on the seat and in the inside leg from the knee. Also, most wore short top boots although a few officers wore the higher Wellington boot and had white canvas leggings (Graham 1986: 346).

1/Lt. King described Brig. Gen. Crook in 1876 as wearing a "worn shooting-jacket, slouch felt hat, and soldier's boots, with ragged beard braided and tied with tape …" (King 1890: 52). Probably referring to officers of the 7th Cavalry, the *Army & Navy Journal* commented: "the true dandy dons a buckskin shirt with an immense quantity of fringe dangling about in the wind" (*ANJ*, August 19, 1876: 22). In emulation of their commander's buckskin suit, officers of the 7th Cavalry, including Capt. Myles W. Keogh and Capt. Tom Custer, wore buckskin jackets and trousers. Recalling the officers in the five companies which Custer led on June 25, 1876, Sgt. Daniel A. Kanipe, of Co. C, recalled that most of the officers who were killed wore regular soldier's uniform as they did not want the enemy to see any rank insignia (Hardoff 2002: 12). Many of the officers in the 7th Cavalry, including Custer, wore the "fireman-style" blue shirt. With no rank insignia, this was double-breasted and trimmed in white or yellow tape, usually with a set of crossed sabers, similar to the cap insignia, embroidered in white or yellow silk on the points of the collar.

Cavalrymen on campaign favored the felt hat. Some men wore the 1872-pattern black folding hat which had japanned hooks and eyes which fastened the brim in position like a chapeau. This hat could also be worn with the brim down as protection, in theory, against the elements. Because of the poor quality of this headgear, however, many men purchased civilian hats which led to a variation in hat color. Regarding hats worn by the 7th Cavalry, Kanipe commented that the soldiers of C Troop, E Troop, and L Troop wore white hats, and the others wore black hats (Hardoff 2002: 12). Whatever style was worn, cavalry hats were usually trimmed with a yellow worsted cord and tassels.

On campaign in Montana Territory in 1876, the 7th Cavalry was armed with carbines and revolvers only. In later recollections, Pvt. Slaper of Co. M wrote: "At the Powder river, our wagons were all sent back. Our sabers were also here boxed and returned; no one, not even an officer, retaining this weapon. The regimental band also was sent back" (*HT*, November 2, 1923: 5:4). During 1875, cavalry regiments began to refit with the .45-caliber Springfield carbine, which had been in production since 1873. Some smaller numbers of altered .50-caliber Sharps carbines were also still in service. Of the units involved in the Indian War of 1876, the 2d Cavalry was armed with 949 Springfields and ten Sharps; the 3d Cavalry had 850 Springfields and 16 Sharps; the 5th Cavalry carried 530 Springfields and 193 Sharps; and the 7th Cavalry had 808 Springfields and 24 Sharps. Problems were experienced with the single-shot Springfields as they tended to heat up and jam after only three shots. Native American eyewitnesses tell of Custer's men under fire on Last Stand Hill trying to dig melted shells from their carbines with knives.

On July 11, 1876, Maj. Marcus A. Reno, 7th Cavalry, reported to Brig. Gen. Stephen V. Benet, Chief of Ordnance, that during the engagement with the Sioux at the Little Bighorn, "out of 380 carbines in my command, six were rendered unserviceable in the following manner … failure of the breech block to close, and leaving a space between the head of the cartridge and the end of the block, and when the piece was discharged and the block thrown

Lt. Col. George A. Custer was renowned for his non-regulation apparel. In this view by an unknown photographer he wears a fringed buckskin jacket with Army buttons attached, buckskin trousers, colorful bandana, and fur cap. During the heat of battle at the Little Bighorn he stowed his jacket over his saddle and fought and died in his shirtsleeves. (Little Bighorn Battlefield National Monument LIBI 00019 00633)

open, the head of the cartridge was pulled off, and the cylinder remainder in the chamber, whence with means at hand it was impossible to extract" (*ANJ*, August 19, 1876: 26).

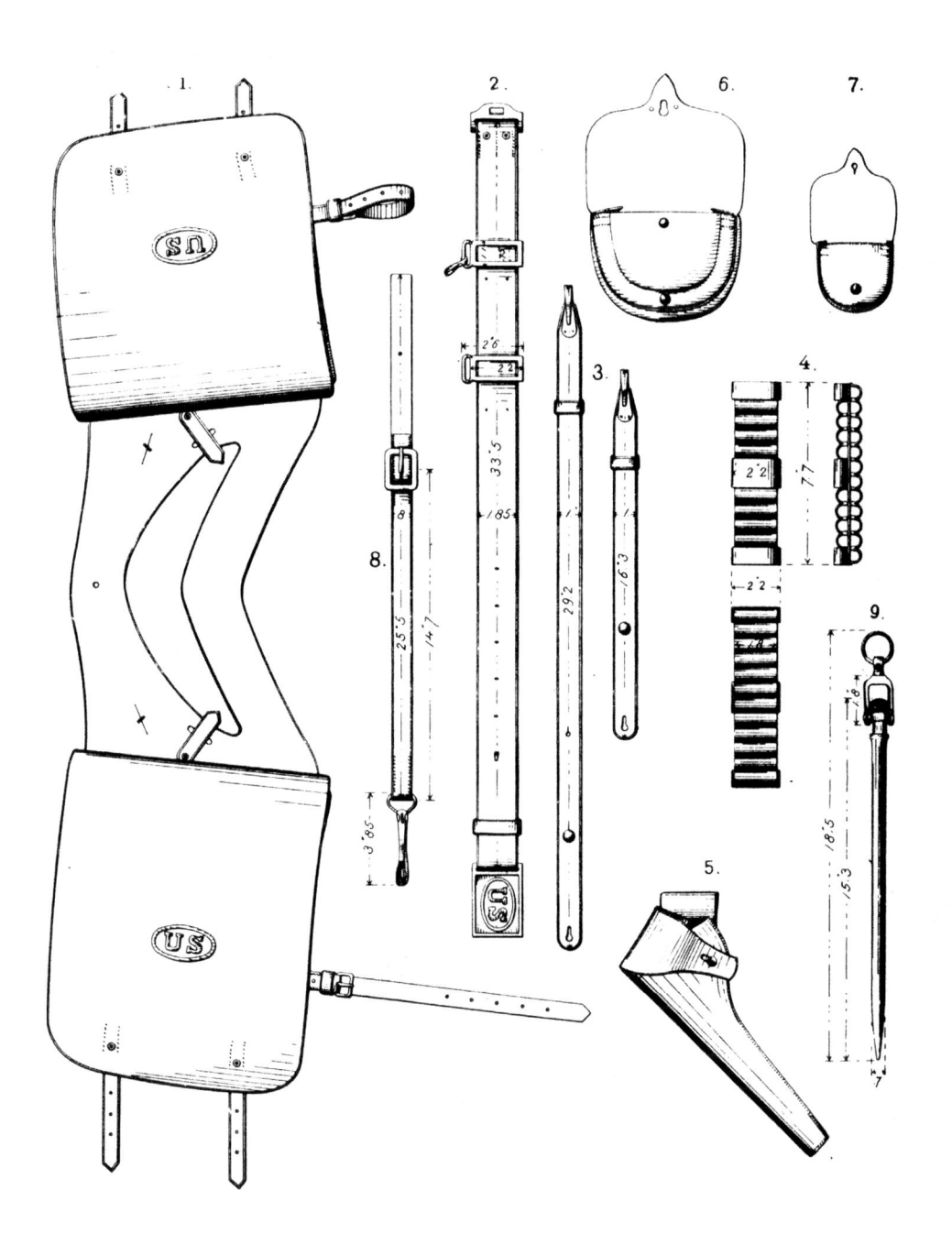

Employing a tactic widely used during the Civil War by Union and Confederate armies, Custer organized the 7th Cavalry into companies identifiable by the color of their mounts. As a result, Co. A rode dark bays, companies. B, F, H, L, and M had light bays, Co. C light sorrels, Co. E grays, Co. K sorrels, while Co. D was known as "The Black Horse Troop." The remaining two companies had horses of mixed colors.

US cavalry equipment is shown in this 1874 plate: (**1**) saddle bags; (**2**) waist belt and plate; (**3**) saber slings; (**4**) movable cartridge loops; (**5**) pistol holster; (**6**) carbine cartridge pouch; (**7**) pistol cartridge pouch; (**8**) link, to support waist belt; (**9**) picket pin. (Author's collection)

CONDUCT IN BATTLE

Sioux

The basis of the Sioux battle-honor system was the coup, which was awarded for touching but not killing an enemy. It was the daring required of close contact for which the honor was given. A warrior's reputation was dependent on the number of touches, hence points, he could accumulate. To "count coup," he might use his hand, his coup stick, bow, lance, or whip. A system of graduated points was evolved whereby the first warrior to touch an enemy was awarded the right to wear an eagle feather upright at the rear of his head. The second warrior to touch the same enemy was entitled to wear an eagle feather tilted to the left. The third won the right to wear an eagle feather horizontally, while a fourth and last could wear a buzzard feather hung vertically. The last three feathers were known as "count feathers." Coup counting was so important that a warrior might mortally wound an enemy with a bullet from his gun, or arrow from his bow, yet gain no count because another Sioux had beaten him to the touch. All coups had to be witnessed and later verified, and a warrior was considered dishonored if a coup was counted on him.

Coups were also recognized for other acts of bravery in warfare. Killing an enemy in hand-to-hand fighting permitted the victor to paint a red hand on his clothing or on his pony. Saving a friend in battle entitled a warrior to paint a cross on his clothing and a double cross was worn if a fellow Sioux had been carried to safety on the back of his pony. Coups might also be indicated by painting vertical stripes on leggings, with red stripes indicating that the wearer had been wounded in battle. Coup feathers dyed red also signified wounds while notched feathers showed the wearer's pony had been wounded. Sioux scouts successful in sighting an enemy were entitled to wear a black feather ripped down the center with the tip remaining.

Coups earned for stealing enemy ponies or horses involved a double reward. Apart from the tangible asset accrued from ownership of an additional animal, the warrior could paint horse hooves on his mount, coup feather or leggings,

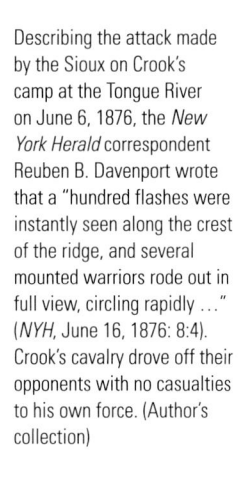

Describing the attack made by the Sioux on Crook's camp at the Tongue River on June 6, 1876, the *New York Herald* correspondent Reuben B. Davenport wrote that a "hundred flashes were instantly seen along the crest of the ridge, and several mounted warriors rode out in full view, circling rapidly …" (*NYH*, June 16, 1876: 8:4). Crook's cavalry drove off their opponents with no casualties to his own force. (Author's collection)

the number indicating how many animals were taken. Taking advantage of the US cavalry skirmish system the Sioux blew whistles and waved blankets in the air as they rode toward the men who held the dismounted troopers' horses, in hopes they would stampede carrying away both extra ammunition and the troopers' means of escape.

The taking of a scalp was important to the victorious warrior. In battle this was a badge of honor, a sign of victory, and a symbol of life, as the Sioux believed that the human spirit dwelled in human hair. When a warrior presented the scalp of an enemy to his women after a battle, he gave not a gruesome trophy, but the very spirit of the fallen enemy.

In battle, both the Sioux and Cheyenne preferred to send forward smaller groups of warriors as decoys to draw the enemy into an ambush or trap, rather than engage in full-on combat. Their skill at concealment in brush and undulating terrain by larger parties of warriors at the Rosebud and Little Bighorn proved this to be a very successful tactic. According to William J. Bordeaux, who passed on accounts of Sioux warriors at the Rosebud battle, their attack was not carried out in a single group but in waves, a fighting style pioneered by Crazy Horse which was sometimes successful in encircling Army forces (Morrison 2010: n.p.n.).

US cavalry

The US cavalry of 1876 used Lt. Col. Emory Upton's *Cavalry Tactics: United States Army – assimilated to the Tactics of the Infantry and Artillery*, which had been officially adopted by the Army via War Department General Order, No. 6, dated July 17, 1873. In his capacity as Commandant of Cadets at West Point during 1870–75, Upton recognized that a unified system of drill and tactics was needed, the commands of which were compatible among the cavalry, infantry, and artillery, so that an officer could move from one branch of service to another and quickly learn the drill of the new unit. His manual also took into account the increasing use of the breech-loading and repeating carbines which would quickly leave the close formations prescribed in previous tactical manuals riddled with casualties.

As a result of the adoption of Upton's tactics, the Army incorporated a "set of fours" as the basic, or smallest, cavalry unit or squad. This was designed to simplify operations, increase speed, and eliminate cumbersome maneuvers. The rest of the hierarchical tactical organization within the regiment remained the same. In ascending order of size and composition, this consisted of the squad (four men), section (two squads), platoon (two sections), company (two platoons), battalion (between two and seven companies), wing (two battalions), and regiment (two wings). When battalions were divided into smaller units these were also referred to as wings.

As directed by Upton's tactics, dismounted skirmishing became the main cavalry mode of engagement with the enemy, which facilitated the dispersal of men on a firing line. Skirmishers could be deployed on the march or at the halt. On the march, they served to clear the way for the main body of troops. This could be performed either mounted or on foot. On campaign and in battle, cavalrymen did not always perform as mounted skirmishers but rather served as mounted infantry. By dismounting and kneeling under fire, the

Load.   Ready.   Aim.

These figures from Lt. Col. Emory Upton's *Cavalry Tactics: United States Army – assimilated to the Tactics of the Infantry and Artillery,* published in 1873, show the drill positions "Load," "Ready," and "Aim" for dismounted cavalrymen. The full-dress uniform is illustrated in these drawings. (Courtesy of John Langellier)

trooper presented a much smaller target for the enemy and could take aim much more accurately.

The preparatory command "To fight on foot," followed by "As skirmishers," required each cavalryman to dismount and deploy along a firing line at 5yd intervals, with 15yd gaps between each set of four men. These intervals could be greater or lesser at the commander's discretion. Odd-numbered skirmishers in each set of four fired a round on command and then reloaded as even-numbered skirmishers fired on order. Each man then continued to fire roughly in an odd-even sequence without regard to the others until the "Cease fire" command was given. Skirmish tactics could be employed by the platoon, company, battalion, or even at regimental level.

Dismounted skirmishing required one of every four men, designated as a horse holder, to remain mounted and control the riderless horses of the other three. Horse holders retired to a safe position in the rear. A reserve force, either mounted or dismounted, was posted about 300yd to the rear of the firing line, and the led horses would be held near the reserve if possible. On campaign, Upton's tactics required defensive squares be formed to protect night encampments, and also to fend off large-scale mounted Native American attacks.

Approaching a field of action, a cavalry regiment usually rode in "column of fours," and moved into line of battle when preparing for a mounted charge, which was still the shock tactic particular to the mounted branch of service. Officers were instructed to order a cavalry charge only over a short distance, in order to keep good control and not fatigue the horses. The men were ordered to draw their weapons, and the line advanced from a slow walk, to a trot, then a gallop, and finally a charge. Contact with the enemy was optimally at 50–75yd (Chun 2004: 65).

The Rosebud

June 17, 1876

BACKGROUND TO BATTLE

On February 8, 1876, Lt. Gen. Philip H. Sheridan, commander of the Military Division of the Missouri, directed Brig. Gen. Alfred H. Terry, commanding the Department of Dakota, and Brig. Gen. Crook, commanding the Department of the Platte, to find and defeat the Sioux and their allies. Terry instructed Col. John Gibbon, commanding the District of Montana, to gather all his detachments and move south and then east from Fort Shaw. Terry would lead a column west from Fort Abraham Lincoln on the Missouri River in Dakota Territory. Crook would march north from Fort Fetterman, on the Oregon Trail in Wyoming Territory.

The column commanded by Crook was the first in the field, leaving Fort Fetterman on March 1, 1876. Crook's command consisted of ten companies of the 3d Cavalry, five companies of the 2d Cavalry, and two companies of the 4th Cavalry, plus three companies of the 9th Infantry. Having placed Col. Joseph J. Reynolds in command of the column, Crook retained overall command of operations. Smoke signals and scouts were spotted soon after Crook began his march. During the second night out, the Native Americans successfully stampeded the beef herd, which deprived the soldiers of their only source of fresh meat. Three days later the Native Americans raided the main encampment, wounding two men.

As a result, on March 5 Crook ordered his infantry, with the train, to return to Fort Reno. Meanwhile, his cavalry, issued with only 15 days' rations, was concealed until dark when it resumed its march. The ruse worked as the Native Americans followed the infantry and for the next ten days the cavalry searched unnoticed for Native Americans. Led by the experienced scout Frank Grouard, they finally found the winter encampment of Crazy Horse and his

Lt. Gen. Philip H. Sheridan wished to conduct the 1876 campaign during the winter, which would find the Sioux and their allies in the worst circumstances. Although the separate columns were designed to catch the Native Americans in a pincer movement, this was never clarified in any set of orders. Moreover, Sheridan's orders did not specify an overall commander for the operation. (US National Archives 111-B-2520)

Commanding the District of Montana, Col. John Gibbon led a column from Fort Shaw in Montana Territory. His command initially consisted of five, later six, companies of the 7th Infantry, plus a Mounted Detachment and Battery containing two Gatling guns and a 12-pdr Napoleon gun. After passing Fort Ellis, this force was joined by four companies of the 2d Cavalry, commanded by Maj. James S. Brisbin, which increased its size to 428 officers and men. (Library of Congress LC-DIG-cwpb-04455)

Entitled "Signal Fires of the Sioux, near Powder River," this engraving was published in *Frank Leslie's Illustrated Newspaper* on August 12, 1876. (Author's collection)

band in the Powder River Valley on March 17. Reynolds was ordered forward to attack, but his labored approach through the snow gave his opponents time to withdraw to the safety of the bluffs. Anxious about being cut off, Reynolds burned the village, destroyed large amounts of ammunition and powder stored in the lodges, and withdrew his command so hastily that he left his dead and wounded behind.

Gibbon's Montana column was the second in the field, departing from Fort Shaw on March 17, 1876. Proceeding alongside the Yellowstone River, Gibbon arrived at Fort F.D. Pease on April 20. At this point, Crook's situation affected the progress of Gibbon's force. As he needed time to refit after the botched Powder River attack, Crook did not intend taking to the field again until mid-May. Thus Terry ordered Gibbon to encamp at Fort F.D. Pease until his movements could be coordinated with those of the other columns. As a result, the whole campaign lost its winter advantage.

On May 16, Gibbon's chief scout, 1/Lt. James H. Bradley, discovered a large Native American encampment by the Tongue River, and the next day Gibbon ordered most of his command to cross the Yellowstone in order to attack it. Unfortunately, the river crossing proved too difficult due to the rising waters. Also, within an hour of Bradley's return a large Sioux war party appeared on the prairie south of the Yellowstone. With only his cavalry across the river before dark, and believing that the Sioux were aware of his movements, Gibbon called off the expedition and returned his whole force to the north bank of the river. Strangely, he decided not to report this aborted action and the presence of the Native American encampment to Terry at this stage. During scouting activity on May 19 and 27, Bradley found further large encampments, but again Gibbon failed to report these.

Meanwhile inclement weather delayed the departure of Terry's 925-strong column from Fort Abraham Lincoln until May 17. Terry's column carried enough rations for a 30-day campaign. Three companies of the 20th Infantry were transported aboard the supply steamer *Josephine* up the Yellowstone River to the mouth of Glendive Creek, where they established a depot containing rations for another 30 days (*NYH*, June 19, 1876: 2:4; *ANJ*, June 3, 1876: 689). Another steamer, the *Far West*, was to set out later carrying a further 30 days' rations.

Terry marched due west and was encamped by Beaver Creek by June 3. He initially expected to find a large Native American encampment by the Little Missouri River and ordered Custer forward with several companies of cavalry to reconnoiter the area. Completing a 50-mile ride, Custer reported that there had been no evidence of the Sioux and their allies in that region for at least six months. In fact, Sitting Bull's main encampment was farther west on the Tongue River.

While at Beaver Creek, Terry received a dispatch from Gibbon that only vaguely referred to sightings of a Native American encampment on the Tongue River. As a result, Terry determined to march southwest toward the Powder River, and sent a courier to Glendive Creek with orders to send supplies by steamer to meet him there. Reaching the mouth of the Powder River on June 7, Terry personally took a boat downstream the next day, in hopes of consulting with Gibbon. Instead, he met up with several of Gibbon's couriers, and finally gained detailed intelligence about the sighting of Native Americans that Gibbon had not previously reported. As a result of Gibbon's lack of communication, Terry took command of both columns.

In the meantime, on May 29 Crook finally set out from Fort Fetterman with a 1,051-man column consisting of 15 companies from the 2d and 3d Cavalry, and five companies from the 4th and 9th Infantry. Crook's train consisted of 106 large Army wagons carrying about 500,000lb of supplies; 600 pack mules carried about 100,000lb of additional supplies. The cavalry rode about 1,200 horses, and fresh meat was provided by a herd of some 50 beef cattle. A pontoon bridge and tackle for a miniature ferry were "embraced in the general equipment" (*SFC*, June 14, 1876: 1:9). Chief Scout Frank Grouard, accompanied by Sioux interpreter Louis Richaud, and Crow interpreter Baptiste "Big Bat" Pourier, moved ahead to recruit Crow warriors as scouts and auxiliaries which were to be waiting for the column at the abandoned Fort Reno.

Crook's column reached the ruins of Fort Reno by June 2. To his dismay, the Crow allies scout Frank Grouard had been tasked with organizing were nowhere to be seen. Despite their hatred of the Sioux, many of the Crow had balked at the offer to serve with the US Army, and were only persuaded to do so after extensive negotiations and an offer of substantial rewards.

Thus, Crook continued the march north without his Native American allies, and by the night of June 5 was encamped at the abandoned Fort Phil Kearny. Setting out again the next day without experienced scouts, the expedition soon became lost. Mistaking the headwaters of Prairie Dog Creek for those of Little Goose Creek, the column proceeded alongside the wrong

Responsible for the Department of Dakota in 1866–69 and 1872–81, Brig. Gen. Alfred H. Terry commanded the three-prong expedition to crush the Sioux and Cheyenne in 1876. Terry's force consisted of all 12 companies of the 7th Cavalry under Lt. Col. Custer; two companies of the 17th Infantry commanded by Bvt Maj. Louis H. Sanger; one company of the 6th Infantry led by Capt. Stephen Baker; a battery of four Gatling guns under 2/Lt. William H. Low, Jr., and 2/Lt. Frank X. Kinzie; and a detachment of Native American scouts led by 2/Lt. Charles A. Varnum, 7th Cavalry. The 7th Cavalry was organized into two wings, each consisting of two battalions, with Maj. Marcus A. Reno commanding the Right Wing, and Capt. Frederick W. Benteen commanding the Left Wing. (Library of Congress LC-DIG-cwpbh-00101)

Based on a sketch by Charles St. G. Stanley, this engraving of Crook's encampment at Goose Creek was published in *Frank Leslie's Illustrated Newspaper* on August 26, 1876, and shows the arrival on June 14 of the Shoshone allies at center led by the Stars and Stripes. To the right is the cavalry camp. (Author's collection)

water course, and by June 7 arrived at the confluence of Prairie Dog Creek and the Tongue River, where it camped for the next three days.

According to a dispatch from Reuben B. Davenport, correspondent of the *New York Herald*, on the night of arrival at the Tongue River the "camp was aroused at twelve o'clock by a loud exclamation delivered by a somber figure walking on the top of the bluffs on the north bank, opposite General Crook's head-quarters. Other figures from time to time appeared, and haranged [sic] successively during an hour. As nearly as could be comprehended they announced the destruction of the invading force if not withdrawn, and warned … of a formidable attack before two suns should roll around" (*CDE*, June 16, 1876: 5:6). As a result, Crook doubled his pickets during the next few days. On June 9, his infantry pickets spotted and fired at some warriors who were in the process of concealing themselves behind rocks on the bluff opposite their encampment. Hundreds of Sioux appeared soon after on the ridge across the river. A volley from the camp was fired into the bluffs, while the beef cattle, pack mules, and horses were secured to prevent them being run off. A half-mile upstream the Sioux made an attempt to cross the river, but were foiled by more pickets. Launching a counterattack, Crook ordered Capt. Anson Mills, commander of Co. M, 3d Cavalry, to lead a battalion of troopers across the river. Dismounting in a grove out of view, they scrambled up a deep ravine to the top of the bluffs where they were deployed in a skirmish line and eventually drove off the Native Americans.

Two days later, Crook led his column 11 miles back up Prairie Dog Creek, and then about 3 miles west to his original destination at the forks

After their arrival at Crook's encampment at Goose Creek on June 14, the Shoshone performed a war dance, beating their scalp-poles against their gun barrels. (Author's collection)

of Goose Creek, where he established a base camp for further operations. On June 14, Grouard finally caught up with the column, bringing with him 261 Crow and Shoshone (or Snake) allies. Among the Crow were the bands led by Old Crow, Medicine Crow, Good Heart, and Feather Head. Soon after, the scout Tom Cosgrove arrived with 78 Shoshone, described by a news correspondent as "the best of the Snakes," who were "well armed and mounted." Most importantly, the Crow allies reported "the Sioux as thick as grass on the south side of the Yellowstone, near the mouth of Rosebud River" (*DIO*, June 21, 1876: 1:6). Crook responded to this news by ordering his entire command into light marching order. Each man was to carry only one blanket, 100 rounds of ammunition, and four days' rations in saddle bags. The train would remain at Goose Creek. The infantry would be mounted on mules.

At 0600hrs on June 16, Crook led his force north out of the encampment at Goose Creek. The column crossed to the north bank of the Tongue River and proceeded downstream until early afternoon when it turned west toward the headwaters of Rosebud Creek. At this point the column encountered a huge herd of buffalo grazing on either side of the trail, and the Crow and Shoshone charged off on a killing spree, despite Crook's best efforts to stop them. Alerted by the gunfire, a small scouting party of Sioux led by Little Hawk appeared on a bluff, exchanged insults with the Native American allies, and disappeared off to report the approach of the column to Crazy Horse. By about 1700hrs, and having marched about 35 miles, the head of the column had reached a marshy area around the source of the Rosebud and bivouacked for the night.

Originally published in *Frank Leslie's Popular Monthly* on October 14, 1876, this engraving depicts Crook's column crossing Goose Creek on June 16 as it set out on its march toward the Native American encampment near the mouth of Rosebud Creek. The main column was led by the mule-mounted infantry of Maj. Alexander Chambers, organized into two small battalions. Commanded by Lt. Col. William B. Royall, the cavalry followed with 15 companies grouped into four battalions, each commanded by an experienced senior captain: Anson Mills, Guy V. Henry, Frederick Van Vliet, and Henry E. Noyes. The civilian contingent brought up the rear. The Crow and Shoshone rode ahead and on the flanks of the column as scouts and skirmishers. (Author's collection)

The Rosebud, June 17, 1876

1 *c.*0800hrs: Crook's column halts to rest the men and animals.

2 *c.*0830hrs: The Sioux and Cheyenne attack.

3 *c.*0830hrs: Randall leads the Crow and Shoshone allies to reinforce the picket line.

4 *c.*0840–0855hrs: Van Vliet with companies C and G, 3d Cavalry, is ordered to secure the bluff to the south and drives the Sioux and Cheyenne off the bluffs, thus securing Crook's rear.

5 *c.*0850hrs: Chambers orders companies D and F, 4th Infantry, and Co. C, 9th Infantry, to advance and hold the low bluffs to the north. Noyes dismounts companies B, D, E, and I, 2d Cavalry, and moves north in support, with Co. A holding horses in the valley.

6 *c.*0855hrs: Evans orders Henry with companies D and F, 3d Cavalry, about 1 mile to the west to protect Chambers' left flank.

7 *c.*0900hrs: Mills' cavalry attack the Sioux left flank and drive them northwest off Buffalo Jump toward the cone-shaped hill, and form a dismounted skirmish line. Royall detaches companies B, I, and L and leads them to the western flank to support Henry.

8 *c.*0910hrs: The Sioux and Cheyenne retreat northwest to the cone-shaped hill and west beyond Kollmar Creek.

9 *c.*0910–1000hrs: Royall reaches his westernmost position. The Sioux and Cheyenne withdraw, luring him up the Kollmar Creek ravine.

10 *c.*1030–1100hrs: Andrews' Co. I and then Foster's 2d Platoon advance farther beyond support range.

11 *c.*1100hrs: Andrews realizes he has extended too far and orders Foster to withdraw, and he rejoins Royall. Crook orders Royall to rejoin him on the ridge, but Royall sends only Meinhold's Co. B.

12 *c.*1115–1230hrs: Realizing he is becoming surrounded, Royall makes several attempts to cross Kollmar Creek and rejoin Crook, but only succeeds on the third attempt, sustaining nine killed and 15 wounded.

13 *c.*1200–1245hrs: Crook orders Mills and Noyes to advance north along the Rosebud Valley in hopes of attacking the Native American encampment. He then orders them to change direction and ride west to attack the Native Americans' rear to take pressure off Royall.

14 *c.*1300–1400hrs: Taking advice from Frank Grouard and Crow scouts, Crook aborts his attempt to advance along the Rosebud Valley and marches back to Goose Creek. The Sioux and Cheyenne choose to retire from the battlefield and head north to their encampment.

Battlefield environment

Indicated by the thick growth of wild roses, or sweet briar, from which it derived its name, Rosebud Creek flowed sluggishly through the valley in which Crook's column halted on June 17, 1876. In his after-battle report, Crook stated: "We were near the mouth of a deep canyon, through which the creek ran. The sides were steep, covered with pine, and apparently impregnable" (quoted in Finerty 1890: 448).

The valley was divided into two almost equal parts by the Rosebud which ran from west to east. When it halted, Crook's force was deployed on both sides of the creek with Noyes' battalion, 2d Cavalry, Chambers' five infantry companies, and the Packers and Miners, on the north bank. The rest of his command, composed of Henry's battalion, 3d Cavalry, the two detached companies of the 3d Cavalry under Van Vliet, and Mills' battalion, 3d Cavalry, was on the south bank. The Crow and Shoshone were ranged in advance and on either flank. Pickets were placed along the foot of the bluffs to the north.

The battlefield to the north of the Rosebud consisted of a series of low bluffs beyond which lay several northwest-facing ravines leading toward a higher range of bluffs which included Buffalo Jump. The terrain was so rough and broken that Crook's cavalry was compelled to fight in small detachments. The ravine along which Kollmar Creek ran became known as "Death Hollow" after the battle.

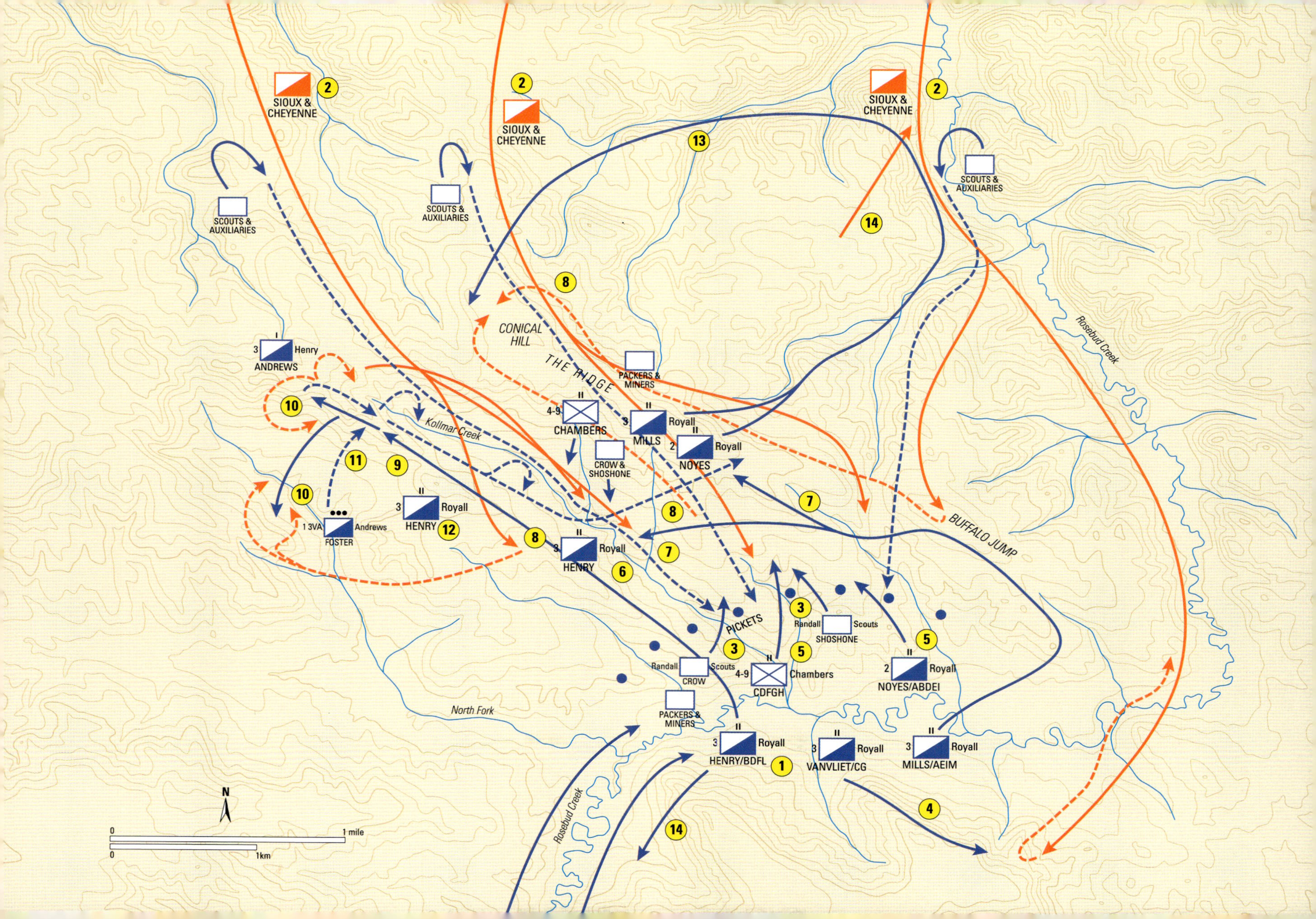

SIOUX & CHEYENNE
SIOUX & CHEYENNE
SIOUX & CHEYENNE
SCOUTS & AUXILIARIES
SCOUTS & AUXILIARIES
SCOUTS & AUXILIARIES
Henry
ANDREWS
CONICAL HILL
THE RIDGE
PACKERS & MINERS
CHAMBERS
Royall
MILLS
Royall
NOYES
CROW & SHOSHONE
Kollmar Creek
Royall
HENRY
Andrews
FOSTER
1 3VA
Royall
HENRY
BUFFALO JUMP
Rosebud Creek
PICKETS
Randall
Scouts
SHOSHONE
Randall
Scouts
CROW
Chambers
CDFGH
Royall
NOYES/ABDEI
PACKERS & MINERS
North Fork
Royall
HENRY/BDFL
Royall
VANVLIET/CG
Royall
MILLS/AEIM
Rosebud Creek
N
1 mile
1km

INTO COMBAT

On June 17, having been roused at 0300hrs, Crook's column was moving again within three hours, heading northward along the south fork of Rosebud Creek. Once again the mule-mounted infantry were at its head but were soon overtaken by the faster cavalry. The high spirits that had prevailed since they had been joined two days earlier by the Crow and Shoshone soon evaporated, for their Native American allies were becoming nervous and apprehensive as they rode around the flanks of the marching soldiers. Although not a single Sioux or Cheyenne had been seen, they seemed to sense their presence. Acting as a correspondent for the *Daily Graphic* of New York, one of Crook's officers commented that "one-half of the route was over a country that for ruggedness and utter sterility almost equals the worst part of the Bad Lands" (*DG*, July 13, 1876: 1:1).

As the column marched north either side of the Rosebud, the Sioux and Cheyenne continued to observe its approach. The 18-year-old Cheyenne warrior Wooden Leg, part of a scouting party watching the soldiers, remembered:

> Heralds in all six of the camps rode about and told the people. The news created an unusual stir. Women packed up all articles except such as were needed for immediate use. Some of them took down their tepees and got them ready for hurrying away if necessary. Additional watchers were put among the horse herds. Young men wanted to go out and meet the soldiers, to fight them. The chiefs of all camps met in one big council. After a while they sent heralds to call out: "Young men, leave the soldiers alone unless they attack us." But as darkness came on we slipped away. Many bands of Cheyenne and Sioux young men, with some older ones, rode out up the south fork toward the head of Rosebud creek. Warriors came from every camp circle. We had our weapons, war clothing, paints and medicines. I had my six-shooter. We traveled all night. (Marquis 1931: 198–99)

After marching about 7 miles, Crook's column halted again at 0800hrs to rest the men and animals. Soon several Crow scouts rode in having seen signs of Sioux up ahead. Reporting to Crook, they suggested that he keep his force concealed in the valley while they reconnoitered farther. At this point Crook made no special effort to post additional pickets, despite being deep in Native American territory, and as they were tired from the previous day's march, the cavalry horses were unsaddled and allowed to graze.

A few minutes later intermittent gunfire broke out in the distance, coming from the bluffs to the north. As the intensity of the gunfire grew, Crow scouts galloped past the head of Crook's column at about 0830hrs shouting, "Lakota! Lakota!" and at almost the same time the Sioux war cry could be heard growing closer. Led by Crazy Horse, the warriors approached in loose column formation with outriders in advance and on their flanks. Of the Native American tactics, the first strategy of the Sioux leader was to attack from the northwest in order to drive the soldiers into the narrow valley at the eastern bend of the Rosebud. When that failed, he lined the sides of the narrow canyon to the north with warriors, intending to lead the soldiers there by feigned retreat.

Of the beginning of the fighting, Wooden Leg recalled: "We found the soldiers about seven or eight o'clock in the morning, I believe. We had slept only a little, our horses were very tired, so we did not hurry our attack. But always in such cases there are eager or foolish ones who begin too soon" (Marquis 1931: 199).

With much of his cavalry unsaddled, and the tail end of his column still arriving in the camp, Crook faced several problems as the warriors attacked. First to respond were his Crow and Shoshone allies, commanded by Capt. George M. Randall, 23d Infantry, who met the first rush of the Sioux and engaged them in bloody close combat for about 10 minutes. These were next supported by dismounted troopers of companies B, D, E, and I, 2d Cavalry, and G and H, 9th Infantry, and the Sioux were momentarily driven off.

By about 0855hrs, the rest of the cavalry south of the Rosebud had saddled up. Waiting for orders, Capt. Alexander Sutorius, commanding Co. E of Mills' battalion, 3d Cavalry, bolstered the morale of his men by assuring them, "It is the anniversary of Bunker Hill, we're in luck!" (quoted in Finerty 1890: 124). Within minutes, cavalry adjutant 2/Lt. H.R. Lemly galloped up with orders from Maj. Andrew W. Evans. With companies D and F of Evans' battalion, 3d Cavalry, Henry was ordered about 1 mile to the west to form a line to prevent the Native Americans from turning the left flank of Chambers' infantry. Van Vliet, with companies C and G, 3d Cavalry, was to seize the high bluff to the south. As Van Vliet reached the crest, he met resistance from the Sioux who had approached from the northeast. Quickly dismounting his troopers, Van Vliet formed a skirmish line and drove them back, thus securing Crook's rear.

At about the same time, Mills' battalion, with Henry's remaining two companies – B and L – attached, was ordered across the Rosebud to charge their opponents' left flank. Moving at a trot in "column by fours" around the rear of the dismounted troopers of the 2d Cavalry, the battalion passed through a gap in the bluffs and debouched into a valley with high ground on either side. Before Mills' troopers could begin their charge, however, Royall caught up with him and diverted companies B, I, and L to the west to support Henry, who was in danger of being surrounded.

Accompanying Mills, reporter John F. Finerty recalled of the charge: "Forward we went at our best pace, to reach the crest occupied by the enemy … We went like a storm, and the Indians waited for us to use our carbines, but several of the men fired their revolvers, with what effect I could neither then, nor afterward, determine, for all passed 'like a flash of lightning, or a dream.'" (Finerty 1890: 124–25). As Mills reached the crest of the first bluff, the Sioux and Cheyenne fell back to farther high ground about 600yd northwest. With his men still mounted, Mills continued his advance as the warriors withdrew to a higher cone-shaped hill. Realizing that the initial charges had done little to weaken the resolve of the Native Americans, Crook sent a courier ordering Mills to dismount his men and throw out skirmishers. Still falling back in the face of the dismounted troopers, the Sioux and Cheyenne continued to snipe from long range. Occasionally, small groups of warriors demonstrated their courage by galloping forward on their ponies to exchange shots at close range, following which they sped away, often unscathed.

Although Brig. Gen. George R. Crook was by training an infantryman, he was an adept cavalry commander. In his recollections of the Black Hills campaign of 1876, 1/Lt. Charles King, 5th Cavalry, described Crook as a "shabby-looking man in a private soldier's light-blue overcoat, standing ankle deep in mud in a far-gone pair of private soldier's boots, crowned with a most shocking bad [white felt] hat" (King 1890: 119). (USAHEC RG77S-Andrew Sheridan Burt Coll.16. I)

Wooden Leg recalled: "Until the sun went far towards the west there were charges back and forth. Our Indians fought and ran away. The soldiers and their Indian scouts did the same. Sometimes we chased them, sometimes they chased us" (Marquis 1931: 200–01). At one point, the Northern Cheyenne chief Comes In Sight charged toward the kneeling troopers, who shot his pony from under him. According to the warrior Little Hawk,

> Many people charged, but one man who had the best horse was in the lead … His horse's hind leg was broken before he reached the soldiers. The Cheyennes retreated toward the hills and left Chief Comes In Sight on foot. He was walking away and all the soldiers were shooting at him as hard as they could. His sister [Buffalo-Calf-Road-Woman] was with the party riding a gray horse. She … saw her brother there and rushed down … and he jumped behind her and she brought him off. Neither was hit. (Grinnell Collection)

As a result, the Native Americans called this the battle "Where the Girl Saved Her Brother."

In the meantime, at about 0910hrs Royall reached Henry with reinforcements. Occupying a low ridge to the northwest of Kollmar Creek, the Sioux and Cheyenne were laying down a suppressive fire into Henry's left flank. Royall advanced all five companies steadily up Kollmar Creek to clear the warriors from their concealed positions. Fighting from ridge to ridge, the Native Americans merely fell back in order to lure the soldiers out of support range.

Photographed by Edward S. Curtis, Crow scouts gather on a hilltop. Brig. Gen. George R. Crook had 261 Crow and Shoshone allies in his column who gave good service during the battle of the Rosebud. (Library of Congress LC-USZ62-110963)

By about 0920hrs, both Noyes' dismounted cavalry and Chambers' infantry had advanced farther north on the eastern part of the battlefield, and soon linked up with Mills' companies on the bluff, which became known as "Crook's Ridge." Joined by companies G and H, 9th Infantry, plus the Packers and Miners, the bulk of Crook's command was formed in a skirmish line around which his headquarters and field hospital were established.

At this point, Crook began to realize his most pressing concern was to the west where Royall and Henry were now in danger of being cut off. By about 1030hrs, Royall had advanced to the head of Kollmar Creek where he dismounted and deployed a skirmish line with led horses held in a ravine. Further taking the bait offered by the retreating Native Americans, Royall ordered Co. I, 3d Cavalry, under Capt. William H. Andrews, to mount up and proceed after the Native Americans as they continued to fall back. In his after-battle report, Andrews wrote that after pushing forward some distance and driving a strong body of the enemy before him, he halted and directed 2/Lt. James E.H. Foster to take the 2d Platoon, numbering 18 men, and clear the ridge on their left from where they were coming under enfilade fire.

After following the retreating warriors for a farther half-mile, Foster realized he in turn was becoming isolated and cut off. As he withdrew to form a defensive position on a bluff, a messenger arrived from Andrews with orders to fall back. Starting at a trot downhill, Foster's platoon got about halfway across a deep dry stream bed when the pursuing Native Americans fired a scattering volley which wounded two enlisted men who clung desperately to their galloping horses. Once Foster had returned to his ranks, Andrews led his men in a dash across a broad valley to rejoin Royall.

Concerned that Royall should return to his main body of troops, Crook sent orders via adjutant Capt. Azor H. Nickerson, 23d Infantry, at about 1030hrs for Royall to withdraw and connect with his left, but Royall sent only Co. B, commanded by Capt. Charles Meinhold, which reached the ridge and joined Noyes' battalion. At this time, Crook also ordered Van Vliet's companies back from their success on the southern bluffs.

Almost completely surrounded by about 1115hrs, Royall next attempted to lead his whole command across Kollmar Creek to rejoin Crook, but came under heavy fire which drove his lead troopers back. Following this he withdrew farther southeast along the ridgeline to another bluff top. With the beleaguered cavalry commander throughout the entire action, an unknown newspaper correspondent wrote that the Native Americans began "pouring upon us a galling fire from three different directions, charging upon our lines and trying to capture our led horses, our men being dismounted as skirmishers" (*ANJ*, July 22, 1876: 801).

Hoping to isolate and overwhelm Royall's retreating force, a large number of Native Americans charged down Kollmar Creek, but their progress was checked by the fortuitous northward arrival of Van Vliet's command as it rode across to rejoin Crook. At the same time, the Crow and Shoshone scouts attacked the flank of the advancing warriors, which threw them into great confusion.

Born in Honolulu, Frank Grouard was a sailor based on the Pacific coast before becoming a stagecoach driver on a route from California to Montana. Captured by Crow Indians, he escaped and wandered along the Yellowstone River where he was found by the Sioux and adopted by Sitting Bull. After living with the Sioux until 1868, he again escaped and made his way to Fort Laramie where he served under Brig. Gen. Crook for $10 a day as a scout and interpreter for the US Army. (Author's collection)

At about 1130hrs, Royall made a second attempt to withdraw from his isolated position but got only part way before being forced to make another stand on high ground to the west of Kollmar Creek. Still in pursuit, the Sioux and Cheyenne continued to attack on three sides, growing bolder by the minute.

Meanwhile, with his immediate perimeter secured and the firing less intense along the ridge, Crook was still determined to press on toward the Native American encampment and, at about 1200hrs, ordered Mills and Noyes, flanked by some of the Native American allies, to advance north along the Rosebud Valley to attack it. Such a move would also hopefully draw pressure off Royall.

At about 1230hrs, Royall decided he could hold out no longer and withdrew his troopers into the Kollmar ravine where they prepared to make a final dash over the 1½ miles of rough open terrain to reach Crook's main position. Around the same time, realizing that Royall's command was in danger of being annihilated, Crook sent a courier recalling Mills and Noyes with orders to head west and fall on the Native Americans' rear.

As the first pair of Royall's troopers set off at a gallop to reach "Crook's Ridge," the Crow and Shoshone scouts charged out to draw the warriors' fire. Crook also deployed two companies of infantry from his main position to charge and provide covering fire from the northeast side of the ravine. Royall's command suffered heavy casualties during their withdrawal, sustaining nine killed and 15 wounded. In fact, 80 percent of total Army losses during the battle of the Rosebud, amounting to ten killed and 27 wounded, were sustained by Royall's four companies of the 3d Cavalry. One of the latter was Capt. Henry, who was described as being "severely wounded in the face, the ball entering near the left temple, and coming out the right side of the face" (*ANJ*, July 22, 1876: 801). Among the attacking warriors at this time was the Cheyenne warrior Young Two Moon, who recalled: "On top of a little ridge the soldiers dismounted again. They tried to hold back Indians but after an officer was shot the body of Indians coming against them was great and troops retreated" (Grinnell Collection).

As the last of Royall's troopers reached Crook's main position, the battalions of Mills and Noyes arrived, but they were too late to be of any assistance. Nevertheless, their unexpected appearance on the warriors' left flank caused the Sioux and Cheyenne to panic and flee. A soldier under Royall later recalled that, by "maintaining successive lines of retreat, aided by the great gallantry of his men and officers," he succeeded, "with loss, in joining Crook's command" (*ANJ*, July 22, 1876: 801).

At last able to concentrate his whole force, Crook led them north along the Rosebud Valley still determined to locate and attack the main Native American encampment. However, scout Frank Grouard strongly advised him not to enter the narrow canyon ahead known as the Rosebud Narrows, stating that the Sioux and their allies were waiting on the high bluffs ready to ambush his entire command, and several of the Crow and Shoshone scouts confirmed that "the Sioux were as many as the blades of grass on the prairies and would destroy them if they entered the canyon" (*ANJ*, July 22, 1876: 806). With much of his ammunition having been expended, Crook reluctantly decided to abandon his expedition and return to his supply camp at Goose Creek, and the battle of the Rosebud was over.

The Sioux warrior Lazy White Bull recalled that the battle at the Rosebud "lasted all day, but when it was over 'Three Stars' [Crook] took his troops and hit the trail back to his base. The Sioux and Cheyennes rode home, leaving scouts behind to watch 'Three Stars' movements" (Vestal 1934: 189). An agency Native American called Kill Eagle spoke with the warriors after the battle, and was told that they had sustained "four dead, left on the field, and twelve that were brought to camp." They placed the wounded at "as high as 400," with 180 horses killed (*NYH*, September 24, 1876: 9:3).

On the morning after the battle at the Rosebud, several Crow scouts found a wounded Sioux warrior crawling toward the creek for water and showed him no mercy. This incident was recorded in *Frank Leslie's Illustrated Newspaper* on October 21, 1876. (Author's collection)

The Little Bighorn

June 25, 1876

BACKGROUND TO BATTLE

At his encampment by the mouth of the Powder River, Brig. Gen. Terry was unaware of Brig. Gen. Crook's fight at the Rosebud; but with information furnished by Col. Gibbon's couriers, he finally had specific, if outdated, intelligence regarding the location of the Native American encampment. He now believed it to be somewhere on Rosebud Creek, having probably been moved farther to the west after its sighting on the Tongue River. Thus, he ordered Maj. Reno to take six cavalry companies on a reconnaissance ride through the valleys of the Powder River, Mizpah Creek, and Tongue River to confirm that the Sioux had not moved east. In order not to alarm the Native Americans supposed to be in the vicinity of the Rosebud, Reno was under no circumstances to venture west of the Tongue. Once his mission was completed, he was to rejoin the rest of his regiment at the mouth of the Tongue River.

Based on Reno's findings, it was Terry's plan to take the Native Americans by surprise. As Crook's column had withdrawn south back to Fort Fetterman, it was hoped the Native Americans would not expect a further attack from the east and north. Hence, Terry's troops would advance southward in parallel columns with Lt. Col. Custer's cavalry on the Tongue and Gibbon's infantry and cavalry on the Rosebud. Having ascended the Tongue at a faster rate, Custer was to turn west to the Rosebud and advance north pushing the Sioux toward Gibbon's column.

During his reconnaissance, which lasted until June 18 and was guided by the interpreter and scout Michel "Mitch" Boyer, Reno did not fully follow Terry's orders. Although he scouted 150 miles along the Powder River Valley, he failed to scout all of Mizpah Creek. Furthermore, after riding only 8 miles along the Tongue Valley, he decided on June 13 to turn west in hopes of finding signs of the Sioux and their allies in the Rosebud Valley after crossing the Tongue–Rosebud divide, which duly happened three days later. Reno's disobedience of orders paid off as when he reached the Rosebud he discovered a very wide lodge-pole trail about 18–20 days old. After following it a short distance, he turned about and traveled all the way down the Rosebud to its confluence with the Yellowstone. He then rode along the south bank of the Yellowstone where he was ordered to halt. His discovery made it clear to Terry that there were no Sioux or allied elements on the Tongue or Powder rivers. The net could now be narrowed down to the Rosebud, Little Bighorn, and Bighorn river valleys.

As soon as Terry received Reno's report, he ordered Custer to march west along the south bank of the Yellowstone to a point opposite Gibbon's encampment at the mouth of the Rosebud. Meanwhile, Terry kept abreast of Custer's column aboard the steamer *Far West*. In consultation with Gibbon and Custer aboard the steamer, Terry changed his plan of action. It was believed that the Sioux and Cheyenne were encamped around the headwaters of the Rosebud, or on the Little Bighorn, 15 miles farther to the west. Custer was therefore to proceed south along the Rosebud Valley until he located the Native American trail discovered by Reno. If the trail appeared to lead to the Little Bighorn, Custer was to continue southward as far as the headwaters of the Tongue, and then turn west toward the Little Bighorn, feeling constantly to his left so as to prevent the Sioux and their allies from escaping south.

Meanwhile, Gibbon's column was to march west along the north bank of the Yellowstone until opposite the mouth of the Bighorn. Accompanied by Terry, the column was then to be ferried across to the south bank by supply steamer, from whence on June 24 it would march up Tullock Creek paralleling the Bighorn. It would then cross to the Little Bighorn valley in hopes of preventing the Native Americans from withdrawing north.

There was great rivalry between the columns, and it was much to Gibbon's chagrin that Custer would seemingly strike the first blow. The cavalry and infantry under Gibbon's command had been in the field since mid-March. As a result, they had come to regard the Native Americans along the Yellowstone as largely their responsibility. Gibbon's column had worked and waited for three months for most of the Sioux and their allies to be concentrated in one area, and for the columns of Terry and Crook to get into position to prevent their escape. Thus, they felt that they ought to be in at the death. Terry's reason for choosing Custer was because his entire 7th Cavalry was

Prior to the battle at the Little Bighorn, Sioux holy man and chief Sitting Bull had a vision in which he saw many soldiers falling upside down into the Native American camp. His people believed this was a prediction of a major victory over the white men invading their land. (Library of Congress LC-DIG-ppmsca-39879)

numerically stronger and would mount a pursuit much more readily than Gibbon's smaller, mixed command.

By noon on June 22, Custer informed Terry he was ready to march. His column consisted of all 12 companies of the 7th Cavalry, and 175 pack mules carrying 15 days' rations of bacon, sugar, coffee, and animal forage. Prior to departure, Custer annulled the wing and battalion organization of the 7th Cavalry, and advised Reno that he would assign commands on the march. During the first day, Custer's column proceeded south along the Rosebud Valley about 12 miles and then camped for the night. During a briefing with his officers, Custer stated that the regiment might encounter as many as 1,500 warriors. Including attached civilians, Custer had 655 men. He also explained that he had refused the offer Terry had made of an additional four companies of cavalry and three Gatling guns because he felt so confident in the abilities of the 7th Cavalry. In fact, the number of Sioux and Cheyenne warriors gathered at the Little Bighorn was a minimum of 2,000. In conclusion he issued orders that no more trumpet calls would be sounded, that the command would move by hand signals, and that there should be no fires except enough to make coffee, until further orders.

Breaking camp at 0500hrs on June 23, the column continued its march for a farther 33 miles that day. At about 0740hrs they came upon an old Native American camp, with a lodge-pole trail about ten days old leading off from it. The column followed the trail along the Rosebud Valley until early evening when it went into camp again. Tasked with carrying dispatches from Custer to Terry, scout George Herendeen recalled: "On the morning of the 24th we pulled out at five o'clock and followed the trail five or six miles, when we met six Crow Indian scouts, who had been sent the night previous by General Custer to look for the Indian village. They said they had found fresh pony tracks and advised that ten miles ahead the trail was fresher" (*ANJ*, July 15, 1876: 791).

During the briefing which followed at 2125hrs that evening, Custer informed his officers that the march planned for 2330hrs would be brought forward and they would move out at once, heading for the divide, and the valley of the Little Bighorn that lay beyond it. His objective was to move the regiment as close to the divide as possible before daylight. Once there, they would remain concealed during the course of the next day, while the scouts located the exact position of the Native Americans' village in preparation for an attack at dawn on June 26. It was Custer's hope that the Sioux and their allies would be caught unawares and sleeping, and that if his regiment was effectively deployed the only avenue of escape would be north toward Gibbon's approaching column.

The night march ended at 0215hrs, and the regiment went into concealment in a wooded ravine. Farther ahead, on the divide or ridge between Rosebud Creek and the Little Bighorn river, at a point later called the "Crow's Nest," lay 2/Lt. Charles A. Varnum and the Crow scouts. In the cold dawn light the scouts, who knew the area, told Varnum that they could see an enormous Native American village and its massive pony herd about 12–15 miles distant. Varnum dispatched a written message to Custer at 0600hrs informing him that the Sioux and their allies had been found.

Custer arrived at the "Crow's Nest" about 0835hrs to see for himself what lay in the valley of the Little Bighorn. Unfortunately, he could see nothing of the Native American encampment, even with the aid of binoculars. However, he did receive some alarming news from Varnum. The scouts had seen two separate parties of warriors riding out toward them, and believed they must have seen the dust cloud the 7th Cavalry had kicked up during their march.

Custer was urged to act quickly and strike out and over the ridge while some element of surprise remained. Returning to his main column, he received more bad news. A five-man detail looking for a box of hardtack lost during the night march had encountered three Cheyenne helping themselves to its contents, and who had swiftly disappeared into the hills. Furthermore, Herendeen had seen two Native Americans not far from the column, who also had fled.

Immediately assembling his officers, Custer informed them that the regiment's presence was clearly known to their opponents, and that they would have to attack at once. He also instructed his company commanders to inspect their troops and detail an NCO and six men to report to 1/Lt. Edward G. Mathey to guard the pack train. The first officer to report back to him would be given the advance in the attack and the last the rearguard. Capt. Thomas M. McDougall, commanding Co. B, was the last officer to report back and consequently his company was detailed to ride with the pack train. Thus, 142 men were now assigned to the rear of the column, moving at a pace of around 4 miles per hour as set by the mules. This meant that almost 25 percent of Custer's entire command would not have any immediate involvement in the forthcoming action.

ABOVE LEFT
The interpreter and scout Michel "Mitch" Boyer, a Quartermaster Department employee of French and Sioux origins, spoke fluent Dakota and Crow. He was assigned from Gibbon to Terry for Reno's scout on June 10, and again on June 22, 1876. It was claimed Sitting Bull offered a bounty of 100 horses for Boyer's scalp. He died near Deep Ravine on June 25, 1876. (Denver Public Library Western Collection X-31214)

ABOVE RIGHT
"Lonesome" Charley Reynolds was chief scout during the Black Hills Expedition of 1874, and would be killed during Reno's retreat from the woodland at the Little Bighorn two years later. (Little Bighorn Battlefield National Monument LIBI_00019_00171)

The Little Bighorn, June 25–26, 1876

MAP KEY

1 *c.*1210–1305hrs, June 25: Custer orders Benteen to begin his scout south of Ash Creek, east of the Little Bighorn, and leads his battalion toward the bluffs, while Reno proceeds along Ash Creek to the Little Bighorn.

2 1322hrs, June 25: Reno crosses over the Little Bighorn and begins his charge down the valley.

3 *c.*1330hrs, June 25: The Sioux and their allies counterattack from the southern end of the encampment as Native American non-combatants seek refuge in a ravine to the north.

4 *c.*1335hrs, June 25: Reno dismounts and fights in skirmish order.

5 *c.*1347hrs, June 25: Custer reaches the bluff at 3,411ft above sea level, sees the size of the Native American encampment, and observes Reno's fight in the valley. According to his version of events, Sgt. Daniel Kanipe is detailed to deliver a verbal message to McDougall to hurry forward with ammunition packs.

6 1400hrs, June 25: Custer descends Cedar Coulee after instructing Cooke to send a written order via messenger Martini ordering Benteen to hurry forward with the ammunition packs.

7 1411hrs, June 25: Becoming surrounded, Reno withdraws to woodland by the river.

8 *c.*1423–1438hrs, June 25: Reno retreats in panic from the woodland and his troopers are pursued across the river. The troopers dig in on what becomes known as "Reno Hill."

9 *c.*1449hrs, June 25: Custer turns northwest down Medicine Tail Coulee to reconnoiter the Native American village and leaves Keogh with companies C, I, and L to cover his rear.

10 *c.*1450hrs, June 25: Crazy Horse leads a contingent north to defend the encampment and protect the Native American non-combatants.

11 1500–1503hrs, June 25: Benteen arrives at Reno Hill.

12 1509–1522hrs, June 25: Coming under fire from encroaching Native Americans, Keogh moves up on to Luce/Nye-Cartright Ridge and then across to "Calhoun Hill."

13 1523–1526hrs, June 25: Custer turns back and re-joins Keogh on Calhoun Hill.

14 1527hrs, June 25: Custer moves to the northern end of "Last Stand Hill" before descending "Cemetery Ridge" in search of a river crossing point from which to attack the Native American village.

15 1535–1635hrs, June 25: Weir rides north to find Custer, followed by Co. D, and reaches "Weir Point." Reno follows after while McDougall arrives at Reno Hill with the pack train.

16 *c.*1542–1546hrs, June 25: After reaching the northernmost ford, Custer meets ferocious Native American resistance and turns back up Cemetery Ridge toward Last Stand Hill.

17 *c.*1600hrs, June 25: Under heavy attack, the remnants of Keogh's men fall back along "Battle Ridge" to Last Stand Hill.

18 1605–1620hrs, June 25: Custer is overrun and killed on Last Stand Hill.

19 1645hrs, June 25: The Native Americans advance on Weir Point and Reno retreats back to Reno Hill.

20 1717hrs, June 25: Godfrey undertakes a successful dismounted rearguard action to cover the retreat to Reno Hill.

21 1725–2100hrs, June 25: The Native Americans surround Reno Hill and attack until nightfall.

22 0500–1900hrs, June 26: After numerous attacks on Reno Hill, the Native Americans set fire to the prairie to cover the withdrawal of their whole encampment north toward the Powder River.

Battlefield environment

The battlefield was dissected by the Little Bighorn River which meandered northwest and flowed into the larger Bighorn River. The vast Native American encampment was located in the valley on the west side of the river and encompassed an area about 3 miles in length and about 1 mile wide. The area east of this river consisted of prairie-covered bluffs interrupted by deep wooded ravines and small streams, including Deep Coulee and Medicine Tail Coulee, which provided drainage from the ridgeline to the river floodplain. Forming an abrupt edge and limiting westward access, certain points along these bluffs offered views across the broad valley and provided defensible high ground for the soldiers of the 7th Cavalry, while the ravines and coulees allowed the Sioux and Cheyenne to advance into the attack out of sight. The bends on the Little Bighorn, which was about 20–30yd wide, made the operations of the 7th Cavalry more difficult and problematic than anticipated. The banks on the west side of the river were steep in places and in 1876 were populated by cottonwoods and bushes which provided some initial cover during Reno's retreat. In 1876 the valley was thick with dust from a drought, while tall sagebrush provided limited cover for the dismounted warriors and cavalrymen.

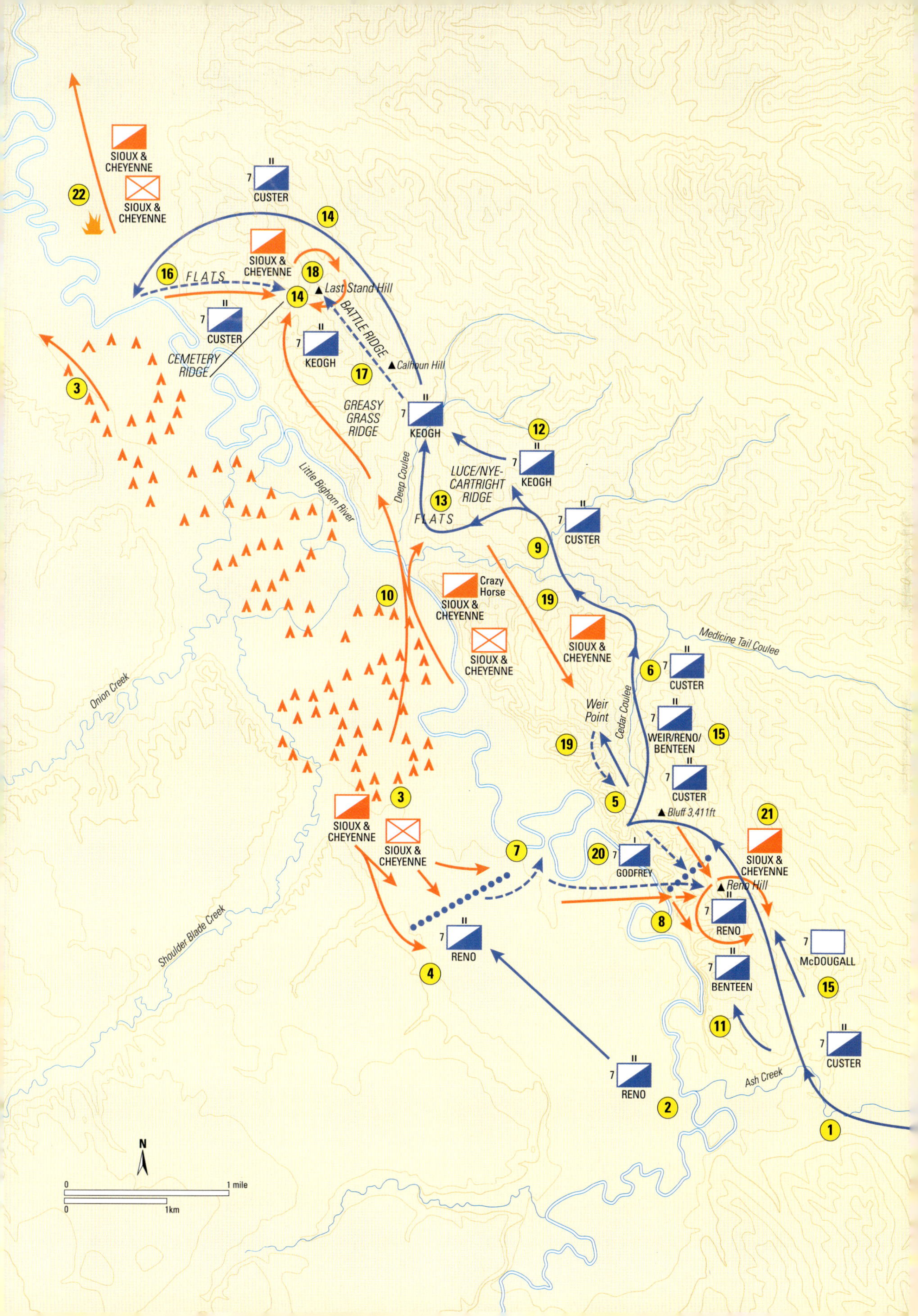
SIOUX & CHEYENNE
SIOUX & CHEYENNE
22
7 CUSTER
14
SIOUX & CHEYENNE
18
16
FLATS
Last Stand Hill
14
BATTLE RIDGE
7 CUSTER
7 KEOGH
CEMETERY RIDGE
3
Calhoun Hill
17
GREASY GRASS RIDGE
7 KEOGH
Deep Coulee
Little Bighorn River
12
7 KEOGH
LUCE/NYE-CARTRIGHT RIDGE
13
FLATS
7 CUSTER
9
10
Crazy Horse
SIOUX & CHEYENNE
19
SIOUX & CHEYENNE
SIOUX & CHEYENNE
Medicine Tail Coulee
6
7 CUSTER
Onion Creek
Weir Point
Cedar Coulee
7 WEIR/RENO/BENTEEN
15
19
7 CUSTER
5
3
Bluff 3,411ft
21
SIOUX & CHEYENNE
SIOUX & CHEYENNE
SIOUX & CHEYENNE
7
20
7 GODFREY
Reno Hill
7 RENO
8
7 McDOUGALL
7 RENO
4
Shoulder Blade Creek
7 BENTEEN
15
11
7 CUSTER
Ash Creek
7 RENO
2
1
N
0
1 mile
0
1km

INTO COMBAT

Leaving the ravine at about 1145hrs, the 7th Cavalry headed west, following the lodge-pole trail leading to the ridge. Deciding to assign commands on the march, Custer retained companies C, E, F, I, and L which continued along the main trail; Maj. Reno, now with companies A, G, and M, marched to Custer's left and abreast; Capt. Benteen, with companies D, H, and K, was sent on a separate mission, at left oblique, to scout in the intervening valleys; Co. B was in the rear with the pack train. 2/Lt. Varnum rode ahead on the left with most of the Arikara scouts. 2/Lt. Luther R. Hare (Co. K) went ahead on the right with Boyer, Herendeen, and the Crow scouts.

In his official report, Reno stated:

> I assumed command of the companies assigned to me, and without any definite orders moved forward with the rest of the column, and well to its left. I saw Benteen moving farther to the left, and, as they passed, he told me he had orders to move well to the left, and sweep everything before him; I did not see him again until about 2.30 p.m. The command moved down the creek towards the Little Big Horn valley. Custer, with five companies on the right bank; myself with three companies on the left bank; and Benteen farther to the left, and out of sight. (*ANJ*, August 5, 1876: 36)

Herendeen recalled: "The scouts were ordered forward ... Our way lay down a little creek, a branch of the Little Horn [Ash Creek], and after going some six miles we discovered an Indian lodge ahead, and Custer bore down on it at a stiff trot. In coming to it we found ourselves in a freshly abandoned Indian camp, all the lodges of which were gone except the one we saw, and on entering it we found it contained a dead Indian [a Sans Arc warrior who had been mortally wounded at the battle of the Rosebud]" (Graham 1923: 311). After setting fire to the lodge, the columns moved on, and scout Fred Gerard rode up on top of a nearby knoll and yelled, "Here are your Indians, running like devils!" (Graham 1923: 312). Encouraged by what was actually false information, Custer resolved to attack as quickly as possible. According to Herendeen, they all "observed heavy clouds of dust rising about 5 miles distant. Many thought the Indians were moving away, and I think General Custer believed so, for he sent word to Colonel Reno, who was ahead with three companies ... to push on the scouts rapidly and head for the dust" (*ANJ*, July 15, 1876: 792).

Reno's report continued: "Custer motioned me to cross to him, which I did, and moved nearer to his column ... when Lieutenant [William W.] Cooke, adjutant, came to me and said the village was only 2 miles ahead and running away. To "move forward at as rapid gait as I thought prudent and to charge afterwards, and that the whole outfit would support me" ... I at once took a fast trot" (*ANJ*, August 5, 1876: 36).

By this time, the Native Americans were well aware of the movements of Custer's force. Hunkpapa Sioux chief Crow King recalled: "Some of our runners went back on our trail ... One came back and reported that an army of white soldiers was coming, and he had no more than reported when another runner came in with the same story, and also told us that the command had divided, and that one party was going round to attack us on the opposite side" (*LWT*, August 18, 1881: 3:2–3). Accompanied by scouts Herendeen and "Lonesome" Charley Reynolds, and with Gerard riding ahead with the Arikara, Reno led his battalion alongside the creek for less than 2 miles until it emptied into the Little Bighorn, and there found a ford. Reno's men crossed the river and deployed on the prairie in line of battle. To the north, about 50 Sioux warriors rode around the loop of the river at the southern end of the camp in order to raise as much dust as possible to cover the flight of the non-combatants. Gerard mistakenly believed the dust indicated a Native American attack and passed back beyond Reno to warn that the Sioux were prepared to fight instead of evading the soldiers. He was met by 1/Lt. William W. Cooke who relayed the message to Custer (Libby 1998: 172). Reno also sent a messenger back to Custer to advise that he had everything in front of him and "they were strong" (*ANJ*, August 5, 1876: 36).

At 1322hrs the Arikara moved to capture Sioux ponies grazing to the west of the camp, and Reno moved forward along the valley, about three-quarters of a mile wide. On the left lay a line of low round hills and on the right the Little Bighorn. In his after-battle report, Reno stated: "I deployed, and, with the Ree [Arikara] scouts on my left, charged down the valley … I, however, soon saw that I was being drawn into some trap, as they certainly would fight harder, and especially as we were nearing their village, which was still standing; besides, I could not see Custer, or any other support, and at the same time the very earth seemed to be growing Indians, and they were running towards us in swarms, and from all directions. I saw I must defend myself, and give up the attack mounted" (*ANJ*, August 5, 1876: 36). Thus, at 1335hrs, Reno issued orders to dismount and form a skirmish line. With one in every four troopers leading horses off to the stand of trees, the remaining 95 men were spread 400yd across the valley to the low bluff in the west.

According to Crow King, the soldiers advanced to within 400yd of the southern end of the camp and the Native Americans "retreated – at first slowly, to give the women and children time to go to a place of safety. Other Indians got our horses. By that time we had warriors enough to turn upon the whites …" (*LWT*, August 18, 1881: 3:3). Within minutes, the entire line was under pressure from hundreds of warriors. Pvt. William Slaper of Co. M later recalled:

> Soon commenced the rattle of rifle fire, and bullets began to whistle about us. I remember that I ducked my head and tried to dodge bullets which I could hear whizzing through the air … We were soon across the stream, through a strip of timber and out into the open, where our captain ordered us to dismount and prepare to fight on foot … Our horses were scenting danger before we dismounted, and several at this point became unmanageable and started straight for the open among the Indians, carrying their helpless riders with them. One of the boys, a young fellow named [Pvt. George E.] Smith, of Boston, we never saw again, either dead or alive. (Quoted in Brininstool 1925: 30)

Forming the firing line, the troopers deployed to the left. According to 1/Sgt. John M. Ryan, Co. M,

Maj. Marcus Reno commanded companies A, G, and M, 7th Cavalry, in the unsuccessful valley charge at the Little Bighorn. In 1879 a court of inquiry exonerated him from charges of drinking and cowardice in the face of the enemy, but he was finally dismissed from the service following court-martial for drinking in 1880. Photograph by David F. Barry at his gallery in Superior, Wisconsin. (Little Bighorn Battlefield National Monument LIBI 00011 7109)

Some of the men laid down while others knelt down. At this particular place there was a prairie dog town and we used the mounds for temporary breast works. We got the skirmish line formed and here the Indians made their first charge. There were probably 500 of them coming from the direction of their village. They were well mounted and well armed. They tried to cut through our skirmish line. We fired volleys into them repulsing their charge and emptying a number of their saddles. Lieutenant [Benjamin H.] Hodgson walked up and down the line encouraging the men to keep cool and fire low. (*HT*, June 22, 1923)

"By this time the Indians were coming in closer and in increasing numbers," continued Pvt. Slaper, "circling about and raising such a dust that a great many of them had a chance to get in our rear under cover of it" (quoted in Brininstool 1925: 40).

Several Native Americans recalled this point in the action. Interviewed in 1877, Sitting Bull stated: "I was lying in my lodge. Some young men ran into me and said, 'The Long Hair is in the camp. Get up. They are firing into the camp" (*NYH*, November 16, 1877: 3:6). According to the Sioux chief Red Horse, "The day was hot. In a short time the soldiers charged the camp … and attacked the lodges of the Uncpapas, farthest up the river. The women and children ran down the Little Bighorn river a short distance into a ravine." (Mallery 1893: 565). Iron Thunder recalled: "I did not know anything about Reno's attack until his men were so close that the bullets went through the camp, and everything was in confusion" (*LWT*, August 18, 1881: 3:4). According to Sioux chief Low Dog, "They came on us like a thunderbolt. I never before nor since saw men so brave and fearless as those white warriors. We retreated until our men got all together, and then we charged upon them. I called to my men, "This is a good day to die: follow me." We massed our men, and that no man should fall back, every man whipped another man's horse and we rushed right upon them" (*LWT*, August 18, 1881: 3:2).

As Reno's troopers neared the camp, the Sioux warrior Little Soldier recalled: "Bullets sounded like hail on tepees and tree tops" (Masters KSHS interview). According to Red Horse, "The soldiers set fire to the lodges" (Mallery 1893: 565). Cheyenne chief Two Moons stated: "I rode swiftly toward Sitting Bull's camp. There I saw the white soldiers fighting in a line. Indians covered the flat. They began to drive the soldiers all mixed up – Sioux, then soldiers, then more Sioux, and all shooting. The air was full of smoke and dust" (Garland 1898: 446).

With two men killed and others wounded, Reno realized he was about to be overrun, and withdrew his whole command back to their horses in the woodland to his right. Meanwhile the Native Americans moved to his left and rear to cut off any chance of retreat to the ford. At this point panic appears to have set in among Reno's men. According to Herendeen, "Reno ordered his men to mount and move through the timber. Just as the men got into the saddle the Sioux, who had advanced in the timber, fired at close range and killed one soldier. Colonel Reno then commanded the men to dismount, and they did so, but he soon ordered them to mount again and moved out on to the open prairie" (*ANJ*, July 15, 1876: 792).

Pressed closely by large numbers of Native Americans the soldiers made a panic-stricken dash across the river toward the high ground beyond. Red

Custer's brother-in-law, 1/Lt. James "Jimmi" Calhoun commanded Co. L, 7th Cavalry, at the Little Bighorn, and was killed while defending the bluff occupied by Keogh's battalion during the latter stages of Custer's attempt to attack the northern end of the vast Native American encampment. The hill was named for him after the battle. (Little Bighorn Battlefield National Monument LIBI 00011 7097)

Horse recalled: "All the Sioux now charged the soldiers and drove them in confusion across the Little Bighorn river, which was very rapid, and several soldiers were drowned in it" (Mallery 1893: 565). Sioux warrior Thunder Bear recollected: "Right among them we rode, shooting them down as in a buffalo drive" (Curtis Papers).

In his official report Reno did not refer to the nature of his retreat, but stated: "I was fighting odds, of at least 5 to 1, and … my only hope was to get out of the wood, where I would soon have been surrounded, and gain some high ground. I accomplished this by mounting and charging the Indians between me and the bluffs, on the opposite side of the river … I succeeded in reaching the top of the bluff, with a loss of three officers and 29 enlisted men killed, and seven men wounded" (*ANJ*, August 5, 1876: 36).

Farther north, Custer continued his ride along the bluffs east of the Little Bighorn. Based on orders given, and information garnered from scouts and couriers, it appears he knew the Sioux were fighting, and intended to support Reno by launching a flank attack on the village. It is possible he intended to take some of the non-combatants hostage which would further draw the warriors' attention. Reaching the top of a bluff 3,411ft above sea level, he gained his first proper sight of the vast encampment, which contained 1,485 lodges accommodating 8,950 people, including the 2,072 warriors involved in the battle (Wagner 2016: 234). He could also see the Native Americans counterattacking Reno, and their elderly and children fleeing, which would have further prompted him to attack the largely unguarded northern end of the village. Sgt. Daniel Kanipe (Co. C) recalled:

> When we reached the top of the bluffs … we were in plain view of the Indian camps, which appeared to cover a space of about two miles wide and four miles long on the west side of the river. We were then charging at full speed … At sight of the Indian camps, the boys of the five troops began to cheer. Some of the horses became so excited that their riders were unable to hold them in ranks, and the last words that I heard General Custer say were, "Hold your horses in, boys, there are plenty of them for us all." (Kanipe 1903: 280)

Originally from the Venetia Province of the Austrian Empire, 1/Lt. Charles C. DeRudio, Co. A, 7th Cavalry, was among 14 men who failed to make their escape from the cottonwoods when Reno's battalion retreated in panic back across the Little Bighorn after the failed charge on the Native American encampment. Remaining undiscovered, he and most of the others managed to re-join Reno on the bluff about 1 mile from the ford later the same day. (Little Bighorn Battlefield National Monument LIBI 00011 7097)

By this time, Custer had decided he needed the support of Benteen's battalion and extra ammunition from the pack train. According to some accounts, he requested his brother Capt. Tom Custer to detail a courier to find Capt. McDougall with the message to hurry the pack train. According to Kanipe, Capt. Custer chose him to deliver the verbal order "If packs get loose, don't stop to fix them, cut them off. Come quick. Big Indian camp" (Kanipe 1903: 280). If Kanipe encountered Benteen, he was to request that Benteen also come quickly. Other accounts dispute Kanipe's version of events and claim he was one of six men who, for various reasons, failed to keep up with Custer's column or fell back to join Reno.

Custer continued his advance northwest and at about 1400hrs reached the head of Cedar Coulee where he ordered Cooke to issue Giovanni Martini (Co. H)

Low Dog

Born an Oglala Sioux *c.*1847, Low Dog or *Sunka Kucigala* became a war chief aged 14 after killing two enemy warriors during an attack on an Assiniboine hunting party. He subsequently led the Oyuhpe band of Oglalas. In 1881 he was described as "a tall, straight Indian, thirty-four years old, not a bad face, regular features and small hands and feet"; at that time Low Dog said that when he had his weapons and was on the warpath, he considered "no man his superior …" (*JWA*, August 19, 1881: 3:2).

Low Dog joined the great encampment by the Greasy Grass River during the summer of 1876. At the beginning of the battle he and his warriors covered the retreat of the women, children, and old folk before advancing to prevent Reno's force from joining Custer. Toward the end of the fight he took part in the final attack on Custer's battalion.

Not friendly toward Sitting Bull, who was not actively involved at the Little Bighorn, Low Dog stated: "If someone would lend him a heart he would fight" (*JWA*, August 19, 1881: 3:2). Before joining Sitting Bull in Canada, Low Dog and some of his band were hunted by the US Army for attacking and killing a mail carrier (*DIO*, June 1, 1881: 2:5). Low Dog, and 20 lodges of his people, surrendered to US authorities at Fort Buford, Dakota Territory, on July 19, 1881. Shipped by steamboat to Fort Yates on the Standing Rock Reservation in South Dakota, Low Dog died there in 1884.

Photographed by David F. Barry at Fort Buford, Low Dog wears a dentalium tooth shell choker and hair pipe breastplate. His braids are wrapped in otter fur and he has a single upright eagle feather in his hair. He holds a pipe-tomahawk with buckskin-wrapped stem. (Little Bighorn Battlefield National Monument LIBI 00011 07142)

---

with a written message to carry to Benteen which stated: "Benteen. Come on. Big village. Be quick. Bring Packs. W.W. Cooke. P.S. Bring Packs" (*CJ*, July 1923: 306). Custer next made the difficult descent down Cedar Coulee and around 1449hrs divided his battalion. Turning northwest he led companies E and F – 89 men – down Medicine Tail Coulee, a dry creek bed in a wide ravine, which provided a route to the river and the village beyond. At the same time, Capt. Myles Keogh was ordered to provide cover and eventually re-unite his three companies – C, I, and L, numbering 121 men – with Custer on what became known as "Calhoun Hill," named after Custer's brother-in-law, 1/Lt. James "Jimmi" Calhoun, who commanded Co. L, to act as a reserve and protect Custer's rear.

The Cheyenne chief Two Moons recalled the arrival of what must have been Keogh's troopers on the bluffs above the Native American camp: "I saw flags come up over the hill to the east … Then the soldiers rose all at once, all on horses … They formed into three bunches with a little ways between. Then a bugle sounded, and they all got off horses, and some soldiers led the horses back over the hill" (Garland 1898: 446). Possibly for reconnaissance purposes, Custer is believed to have descended Medicine Tail Coulee to about one-quarter of a mile from the Little Bighorn but at 1526hrs turned back to

Daniel A. Kanipe

Born in Marion, McDowell County, North Carolina, on April 15, 1853, Kanipe enlisted in the Army at Lincolnton, North Carolina, on August 7, 1872; he was described as being 5ft 11in tall with hazel eyes, light hair, and fair complexion. Assigned to Troop C, 7th Cavalry, he took part in the Yellowstone Expedition of 1873 and the Expedition of 1874 which led to the discovery of gold in the Black Hills.

According to Kanipe, during the battle of the Little Bighorn he was detailed to deliver a verbal message to Capt. Thomas M. McDougall to hurry forward the pack train with extra ammunition. As McDougall claimed he never saw Kanipe until he reached Reno's hilltop defenses, the sergeant may have been one of several men who for various reasons failed to keep up with Custer's battalion.

Kanipe married Missouri Ann, or Annie Missouri, the widow of 1/Sgt. Edwin Bobo, on April 12, 1877. On August 7, 1877, he was discharged from the Army at Fort Totten, Dakota Territory, being described as "1 Sergt Character Excellent" (US National Archives, M233, Army Register of Enlistments, 1798–1914: Registers of Enlistments 1871–1877, H–O: 198). Returning to McDowell County, he worked for the Internal Revenue Service, and was treasurer of the Mystic Tie Lodge No. 237 in Marion for more than 20 years. He also served as captain of the North Carolina Militia Home Guards during World War I. He died, age 73, on his farm on July 18, 1926 (*ACT*, January 14, 1923: 13:1).

This picture of Sgt. Daniel A. Kanipe in full dress appeared in "A New Story of Custer's Last Battle" in *Contributions to the Historical Society of Montana*, 1903. (Author's Collection)

re-join Keogh on Calhoun Hill. He then led his two companies northwest and down the slope off what was later named "Cemetery Ridge" in search of another crossing point farther downstream.

Meanwhile, Crazy Horse's contingent left the Reno fight and turned their attention north. As this group approached Calhoun Hill in vast numbers, 2/Lt. Henry M. Harrington led Co. C in a mounted charge down "Calhoun" coulee, but his 37 troopers were quickly overrun and fell back in panic. Calhoun and 2/Lt. John J. Crittenden fell mortally wounded and Keogh was killed on the eastward slope of "Battle Ridge." Forced off Calhoun Hill, the remains of his battalion withdrew northwest along the ridge to a hilltop today called "Last Stand Hill." Gun casings found by archeologists in this part of the battlefield were bunched together, which is consistent with men losing their skirmish line formation and breaking up in confusion. Overwhelmed by superior numbers, the troopers appear to have fled in panic.

Although Custer approached another ford about a half-mile farther downstream and probably saw the fleeing non-combatants, he turned back in the face of growing resistance from warriors who were furiously defending their women, children, and elderly. According to Sitting Bull, his troopers

RIGHT
Italian-born orderly-trumpeter and messenger Giovanni Martini, aka John Martin, was attached to Co. H, 7th Cavalry, at the Little Bighorn. As Custer led his battalion to the northern end of the Native American village, Martini was dispatched with an urgent note for reinforcements and ammunition, and survived the battle after joining Reno's beleaguered men. He remained in the Army, reaching the rank of sergeant, until age limitations forced his retirement in 1904. Photographed by David F. Barry at Fort Lincoln c.1895, he wears his campaign and marksman medals and has service stripes on the sleeves of his coat. (Little Bighorn Battlefield National Monument LIBI 00019 00192)

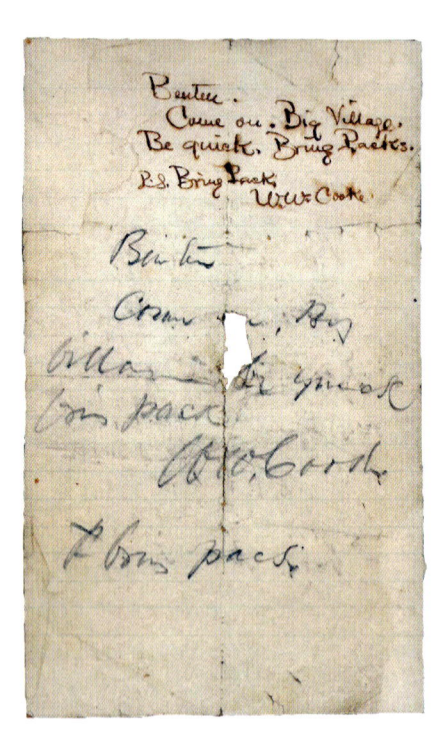

FAR RIGHT
The note hurriedly written by 1/Lt. William W. Cooke contained Custer's last known order. Realizing he faced superior numbers, Custer ordered Capt. Frederick W. Benteen to hurry forward with packs containing extra ammunition. The fact that he repeated "Bring Packs" as a postscript emphasized the urgency of the situation. The smaller script at the top was added by Benteen after the battle. (West Point Museum Collection, United States Military Academy)

looked "exhausted and their horses bothered them so much that they could not take good aim. Some of their horses broke away from them and left them to stand and drop and die. When the Long Hair, the General, found that he was so outnumbered and threatened on his flanks, he took the best course he could have taken. The bugle blew. It was an order to fall back. All the men fell back fighting and dropping" (*NYH*, November 16, 1877: 4:1).

Elsewhere, Reno's battalion continued to dig in on the hilltop it had retreated to at about 1430hrs. Meanwhile, Benteen had found no sign of opposition in his sweep to the south and swung his column back toward the Little Bighorn, to be met by Martini and, presumably, Kanipe. Each bore a similar message, although only Martini delivered the written one jotted down on a page torn from Cooke's pocket book. Martini also mentioned that the Native Americans were "skedaddling," which possibly convinced Benteen there was no need to hurry ammunition packs forward. Instead, he continued toward the gunfire on the bluffs, finally joining forces with Reno at about 1500hrs (Graham 1986: 180). Co. B and the pack train finally reached Reno by 1617hrs which increased his command to 13 officers and 380 men.

In the meantime, Custer had withdrawn under great pressure to Cemetery Ridge where he further divided his command, sending Capt. George W.M. Yates with Co. F (38 men) to head off Native Americans infiltrating up Deep Ravine, while Co. E and headquarters (49 men under 1/Lt. Algernon E. Smith), remained on the ridge. The pressure now became so severe that Custer was overrun and what remained of his contingent was forced back to join Keogh's command on Last Stand Hill. By the time Custer arrived on the hill, only about 40–50 of his 210 men remained, with hundreds of Sioux and Cheyenne swirling around them.

Red Horse later stated that Custer's troops made "five different stands." In each, combat seems to have begun and ended within about ten minutes. Low Dog stated: "As we rushed upon them the white warriors dismounted to fire, but they did very poor shooting. They held their horses [*sic*] reins on one arm while they were shooting, but their horses were so frightened that they pulled the men all around, and a great many of their shots went up in the air and did us no harm. The white warriors stood their ground bravely" (*LWT*, August 18, 1881: 3:2). A Sioux warrior named Hump recalled: "The first dash the Indians made my horse was shot from under me and I was wounded – shot above the knee, and the ball came out at the hip, and I fell and lay right there. The rest of the Indians kept on horseback, and I did not get in the fight" (*LWT*, August 18, 1881: 3:3).

Leading his band of about 80 warriors, Crow King recalled: "We rushed our horses on them. At the same time warriors rode out on each side of them and circled around them until they were surrounded. When they saw that they were surrounded they dismounted. They tried to hold on to their horses, but as we pressed closer they let go their horses. We crowded them … and killed them all. They kept in good order and fought like brave warriors as long as they had a man left" (*LWT*, August 18, 1881: 3:3). Tribal storytellers later spoke of how Buffalo-Calf-Road-Woman may have struck the blow that knocked Custer off his horse following which he died of gunshot wounds (*HIR*, June 28, 2005). About the same time as Custer fell, his brother Tom was shot dead to his left. A few minutes earlier, their younger brother Boston Custer, who had joined the expedition as a guide, forager, and packer, and his nephew Autie Reed, who had signed on as a "herder," had been killed farther down the hill.

This ledger drawing was produced by Red Horse, a Sioux chief, who was present at the southern end of the Native American encampment by the Little Bighorn when Reno made his charge. His drawing depicts Custer's cavalry troopers being pursued and cut down out of their saddles by Native American warriors. Note the naked and mutilated bodies of those already killed. (National Anthropological Archives, Smithsonian Institution, NAA INV 08569500)

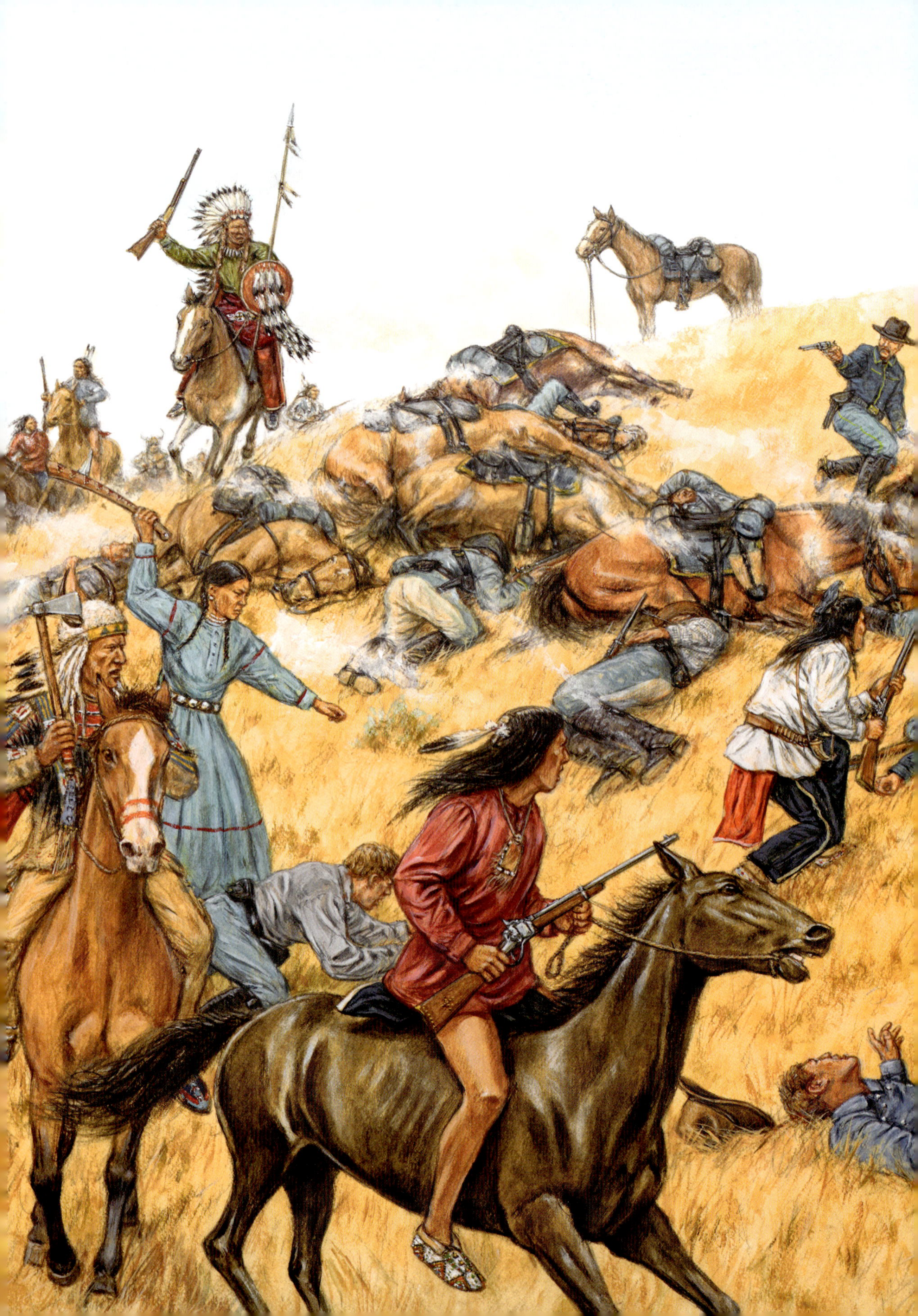

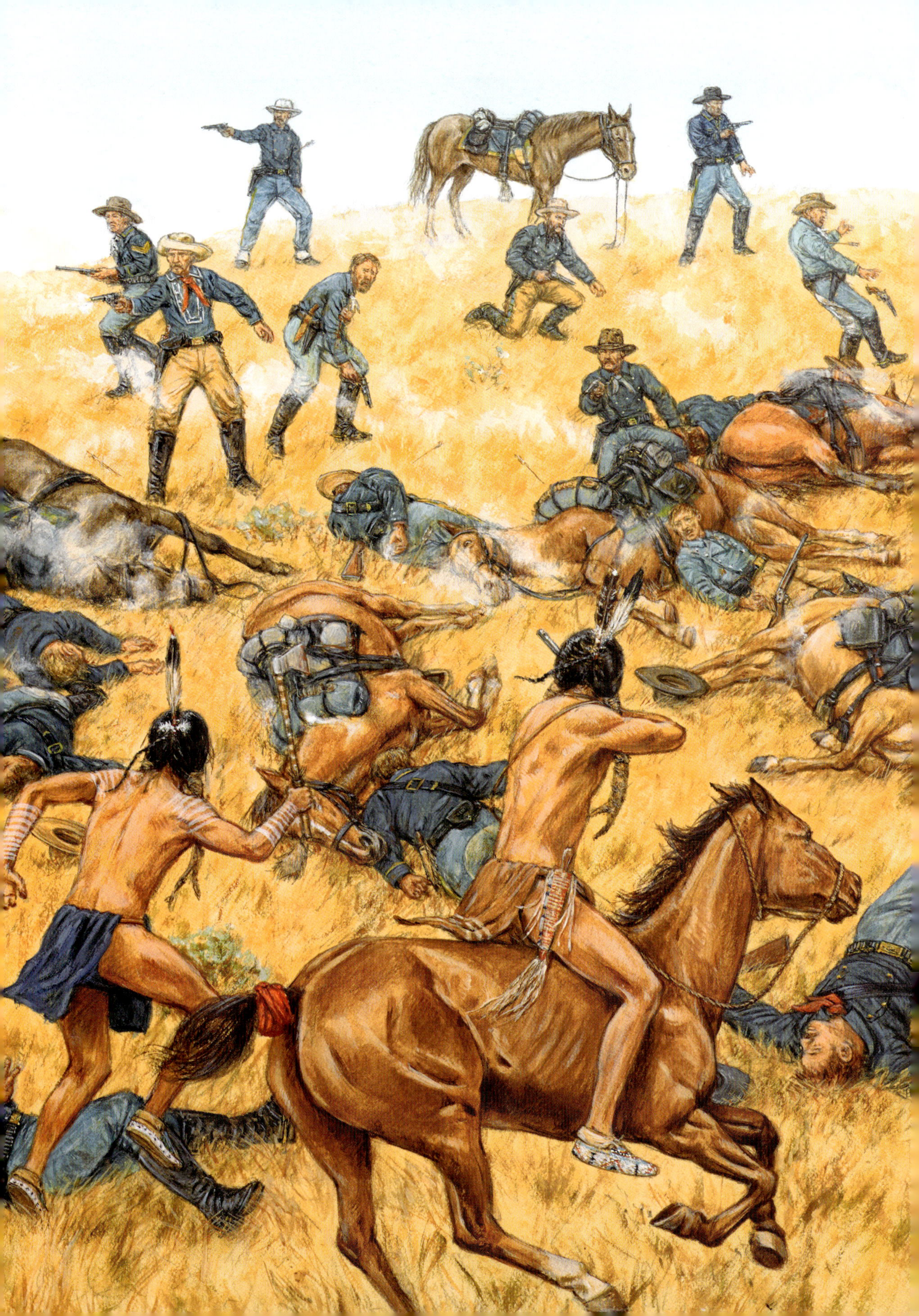

Last Stand Hill

Seen through the eyes of a Sioux brave, the warriors of Crazy Horse make a final attack on the survivors of Custer's battalion, who attempt to defend themselves on a knoll east of the Little Bighorn River that forever after would be known as "Last Stand Hill." The exhausted cavalry troopers rally behind Lt. Col. George A. Custer. His brother, Capt. Tom Custer, 1/Lt. William W. Cooke, and 2/Lt. William Van Wyck Reily, are close by. Having tied his buckskin jacket to his saddle pack, Custer fights in his shirtsleeves as he bellows encouragement to his men, and fires desperately at the warriors closing in for the final kill. Covered in dust and shrouded in gun smoke, some of the troopers attempt to shelter behind dead and wounded horses which encircle the hilltop. A few still hold their horse by the bridle while frantically attempting to load and fire their Springfield carbines or Colt revolvers. Those without loaded weapons use them as clubs as the melee grows more intense.

A Sioux warrior named Little Buck Elk said the Native Americans were "as thick as bees at the fight, and that there were so many of them that they could not all take part in it" (*ANJ*, October 21, 1876: 165). Intent on avenging the death of his two wives and three children during the Reno fight, the Sioux warrior Gall is at the forefront of the attack wielding an axe and wearing only a dark-blue breechclout, beaded moccasins, and hair in otter skin braid wraps topped with a single eagle feather. Wearing her everyday calico dress, Buffalo-Calf-Road-Woman swings a war club at the nearest white soldier. Others, including Cheyenne and Arapaho braves, wear deerskin war shirts, calico shirts, and buckskin leggings. Several have sacred trailer war bonnets, some of which are horned, while others have single and double coup feathers. Weaponry consists of firearms including Winchester and Henry carbines, and Colt revolvers, plus bows and arrows, bow-lances, clubs, and knives.

OPPOSITE LEFT
Although probably photographed by Orlando S. Goff, this *c.*1874 image was copyrighted by David F. Barry (as indicated by the imprint) and shows Capt. Frederick W. Benteen in full-dress uniform. Benteen served in the Nez Perce campaign of 1877, and was promoted major in the 9th Cavalry in December 1882. In 1887, he was suspended for drinking and disorderly conduct at Fort DuChesne, Utah. Convicted and facing dismissal from the Army, his sentence was reduced by President Grover Cleveland to a one-year suspension. Benteen retired from the service on July 7, 1888, citing disability from heart disease and rheumatism. He was brevetted brigadier general on February 27, 1890 for his actions at the battle of the Little Bighorn and in the Nez Perce campaign. (Little Bighorn Battlefield National Monument LIBI 00011 7096)

Archeological evidence suggests that toward the end, and probably shortly before Custer's death, about 30 troopers of Co. E attempted to break out, some on foot, others on horseback, in a desperate attempt to escape. In a matter of 10 minutes or so all were killed as the warriors rushed after them, cutting, stabbing, and clubbing them to death.

Farther south, Reno was in a state of shock as a result of the galling punishment his battalion had taken, and was reluctant to go to Custer's assistance. On joining Reno, Benteen was similarly indecisive. In a letter dated August 7, 1876, 1/Lt. Edward S. Godfrey, commanding Co. K of his battalion, wrote: "As soon as dispositions were made on the bluff, [Capt. Thomas B.] Weir's company [D] was sent to look for Gen. Custer" (*ANJ*, September 2, 1876: 58). In his official report dated August 5, 1876, Reno stated that Weir's company was ordered forward "to open communication with the other command" (*ANJ*, August 5, 1876: 836). In a later narrative of events, Benteen claimed he did not notice that Weir had acted on his own initiative, but promptly followed after him having left the wounded and pack train on the bluff guarded by McDougall's Co. B (Graham 1986: 181).

In fact, Weir rode north with only his orderly, and his second in command 2/Lt. Winfield S. Edgerly mistook this as confirmation that he could follow on with the rest of Co. D. Weir rode about 1¼ miles and by about 1550hrs had reached a promontory which became known as "Weir Point," from where he could see in the distance warriors shooting at prostrate figures on the ground. What he most likely witnessed was some of the closing stages of Custer's defense of Last Stand Hill.

About 20 minutes after Weir left them, and as the head of McDougall's pack train began arriving, Reno and Benteen set out north with companies A, G, H, M, and K. Reaching Weir Point by about 1620hrs, Reno consolidated his advanced position by posting Capt. Thomas H. French's Co. M facing north, and Co. K, under Godfrey, along the ridge facing the river, while companies A, G, and H were held in reserve. In response to a message from Reno instructing him to push on and make contact with Custer, Weir sent word back via 2/Lt. Hare that he could go no farther, and that the Sioux were beginning to surround him. With further confirmation from Benteen that the warriors were approaching in numbers, Reno ordered a rapid withdrawal. Godfrey recalled the minutes prior to this:

> Busying myself with posting my men, giving direction about the use of ammunition, etc., I was a little startled … that the command was out of sight. At this time Weir's and French's troops were being attacked. Orders were soon brought to me by Lieutenant Hare … to join the main command. I had gone some distance … when, looking back, I saw French's troop come tearing over the bluffs, and soon after Weir's troop followed in hot haste … The Indians almost immediately followed to the top of the bluff, and commenced firing into the retreating troops, killing one man, wounding others and several horses. They then started down the hillside in pursuit. I at once made up my mind that such a retreat and close pursuit would throw the whole command into confusion, and, perhaps, prove disastrous. I dismounted my men to fight on foot, deploying as rapidly as possible without waiting for the formation laid down in the tactics. (Godfrey 1892: 374)

The fire from Godfrey's Co. K forced the Sioux to withdraw and take cover, and due to his rearguard action, the rest of Reno's command was able to reach the relative safety of their defended hilltop, arriving only minutes before their opponents. Reno mentioned nothing of Godfrey's action in his report, merely stating: "I dismounted the men, had the horses and mules of the pack train driven together in a depression, put the men on the crests of the hills … and

ABOVE RIGHT
Sioux chief Gall lost two wives and several children at the Little Bighorn when Reno attacked the southern end of the encampment. He was one of the first to realize that another attack was about to be launched in the north and rallied hundreds of warriors for a counterattack which drove Custer back into the bluffs. (US National Archives 111-82572)

ABOVE LEFT
Capt. Tom Custer served as *aide-de-camp* to his older brother George and died with him on Last Stand Hill. Tom Custer's remains were identified by a recognizable tattoo of his initials on his arm. (Little Bighorn Battlefield National Monument LIBI 00197)

ABOVE RIGHT
Pvt. John W. Burkman, Co. L, 7th Cavalry, was Custer's "striker," or personnel orderly. He survived the Little Bighorn, being left behind with the pack train to look after "Dandy," Custer's favorite horse, and eventually becoming one of the 380 enlisted men on the hilltop commanded by Reno. (Little Bighorn Battlefield National Monument LIBI 00019 00175)

had hardly done so, when I was furiously attacked; this was about 6 p.m.; we held our ground with the loss of 18 enlisted men killed and 46 wounded until the attack ceased, about 9 p.m." (*ANJ*, August 5, 1876: 36). Crow King was among the Sioux who attacked Reno and recalled: "We fired at them until the sun went down. We surrounded them and watched them all night" (*LWT*, August 18, 1881: 3:3).

As soon as it was dark, Reno ordered the packs and saddles taken off the horses and mules and used as breastworks. Dead animals were also added to the defenses. Some of the troopers dug rifle pits with knives, and all slept on their arms as best they could. According to Reno, "All this night the men were busy, and the Indians holding a scalp dance underneath us in the bottom, and in our hearing. On the morning of the 26th, I felt confident that I could hold my own, and was ready as far as I could be, when, at daylight … I heard the crack of two rifles; this was the signal for the beginning of a fire I have never seen equalled [*sic*]" (*ANJ*, August 5, 1876: 36). Having rejoined Reno at about 1700hrs during the first day of battle, scout George Herendeen recalled: "The Indians charged our position three or four times, coming up close enough to hit our men with stones, which they threw by hand" (*ANJ*, July 15, 1876: 792). Reno's report continued:

The fire did not slacken until about 9.30 a.m., and then we discovered that they were making a last desperate attempt, and which was directed against the lines held by companies H and M; in this attack they charged close enough to use their bows and arrows, and one man, lying dead within our lines, was touched by the 'coup stick' of one of the foremost Indians. When I say the stick was only about 10 or 12 feet long, some idea of the desperate and reckless fighting of these people may be understood. (*ANJ*, August 5, 1876: 36).

As the day grew warmer, the lack of water became a serious problem, especially for the wounded lying without cover in the hot sun. Following a plea from Dr. Henry R. Porter, the only surviving physician with the command, Benteen asked for volunteers to go for water. A party of troopers made their way down a deep ravine to the river, their movement covered by sharpshooters, and succeeded in bringing water back for the wounded.

By late afternoon, the Native Americans appeared to be losing interest in the battle. Frustrated by their inability to finish off the rest of the soldiers and apparently satisfied with what they had accomplished, they began to withdraw. Crow King recalled: "a chief from the Uncpapas called our men off. He told them those men had been punished enough, that they were fighting under orders, that we had killed the great leader and his men in the fight the day before, and we should let the rest go home" (*LWT*, August 18, 1881: 3:3).

While some warriors kept the soldiers pinned, those in the valley packed up their lodges and set the prairie afire to cover their withdrawal and hinder any pursuit. At approximately 1900hrs, Reno's men saw the huge band move upriver toward a new campsite in the Bighorn Mountains. Although unmolested following the Native Americans' withdrawal, Reno stayed in his hilltop location during the night of June 25/26. The following morning, Terry's column arrived and informed Reno and Benteen of Custer's fate.

Casualties among the Native Americans at the Little Bighorn are difficult to assess. According to Two Moons, "Next day [June 26] four Sioux chiefs and two Cheyennes and I … went upon the [Custer] battlefield to count the dead. One man carried a little bundle of sticks. When we came to dead men, we

This detail from a painting on muslin by White Bird, a chief and headman of the Cheyenne Crazy Dogs warrior society, who fought at the Little Bighorn, shows his version of the end result of Custer's fight on Last Stand Hill. Lying dead toward the bottom of the group, Custer is inaccurately represented wearing his buckskin coat. (West Point Museum Collection, United States Military Academy)

Carried by Co. C, 7th Cavalry, this guidon was found by Sgt. Ferdinand Culbertson who was with a burial party on Last Stand Hill three days after the massacre of Custer's battalion at the Little Bighorn. (Little Bighorn Battlefield National Monument LIBI_00049_01203)

took a little stick and gave it to another man, so we counted the dead. There were 388. There were thirty-nine Sioux and seven Cheyennes killed and about a hundred wounded …" (Garland 1898: 448).

The official list for the 7th Cavalry killed during the battle, including Custer, amounted to 256 officers and men, plus two civilians, five quartermaster employees, two Arikara scouts, and one packer. A further five enlisted men died shortly after the battle. Medals of Honor were awarded to 15 of the troopers of the Reno force who volunteered to fetch river water for the thirsty defenders on June 26. Four sharpshooters who provided covering fire for the 15 troopers also received medals. Strangely, a sixteenth water carrier, the only trooper wounded during the successful foray down to the river, was not awarded a Medal of Honor.

Custer's personal scout, Bloody Knife was detailed to Reno at the Little Bighorn and died in the cottonwoods from a shot to the head during the retreat from the valley charge. (US National Archives 106-YX-84A)

Slim Buttes

September 9–10, 1876

BACKGROUND TO BATTLE

Following the debacle at the Little Bighorn, Brig. Gen. Crook remained encamped at Goose Creek, and Brig. Gen. Terry fell back with his command to his supply base on the Yellowstone River. Both forces waited for reinforcement and supplies. The two armies were not more than 125 miles apart, yet communication between them was extremely difficult as the intervening country was filled with Sioux. The warriors of Sitting Bull and Crazy Horse lay uneasily between the two commands, warily watching them. Observing the approach of strong reinforcements to both armies, they proceeded to get their women and children out of the way, sending them eastward and preparing to do likewise themselves when the time came.

By the beginning of August 1876, Crook had received reinforcements composed of five companies of the 2d Cavalry, ten companies each of the 3d and 5th Cavalry, and ten companies from the 4th, 9th, and 14th Infantry, giving him 1,490 cavalrymen, 400 infantry, and 250 Native American scouts, amounting to a total of 2,140 men. Several days later, Terry's command was reinforced by troops from the 2d Cavalry, plus the 7th, 22d, and 17th Infantry. Crook set out to rendezvous with Terry on August 5, and Terry began his march three days later.

Crook marched north to the Tongue River and then past the campsite where he had been attacked on June 9. Continuing another 30 miles northeast, he then turned to the north and crossed the Panther Mountains to Rosebud Creek. After initially mistaking each other for the enemy, the two columns met on August 10. With a total strength of about 4,000 men, this ponderous force proceeded down the Rosebud following the

Sioux trail which the *Army & Navy Journal* of September 2 reported to be nearly 2 miles wide and "the heaviest ever seen on the plains" (*ANJ*, September 2, 1876: 54). This trail finally separated with one party heading south, possibly toward the Indian agencies, and the other north toward the British possessions.

The two commanders now failed to agree how next to proceed, but settled on a compromise. Terry would march north deeper into his Department of Dakota, but by September 8 he had achieved little success and disbanded his column. Meanwhile, with his Big Horn and Yellowstone Expedition, Crook followed those Native Americans most likely to turn south toward his Department of the Platte. He marched due east on August 22 in one last effort to salvage something from the campaign before another harsh winter set in. The southern Native American trail headed for the Powder River and then diverged from its east bank about 20 miles from its mouth on the Yellowstone. It then went south again toward the Little Missouri River in Dakota Territory.

Significantly, Miniconjou chief Red Horse recalled of this part of the campaign:

> After the Greasy Grass Creek fight we all moved east ... The Indians decided after this fight that there was nothing to be gained by fighting two large bodies of troops, but that there was something gained by having them follow us until their horses gave out, for then they could do us no harm. When the two commands divided we made a stand for one of them, but for some reason they passed us and did not attack us. I left the main camp then with forty-eight lodges and camped at Slim Buttes. (Sioux War Papers, National Archives)

Hinting at appalling weather conditions, Many Shields, a Sans Arc Sioux with the main body of warriors, commented: "The trail of the cavalry passed within seven miles of this large camp but they say from all appearances it must have been raining at the time" (Sioux War Papers, National Archives)

Reaching the headwaters of the Heart River by September 5, Crook reported to Lt. Gen. Sheridan that the trail he had followed had scattered until it could be pursued no farther. With only 2½ days' rations remaining, and his command suffering from hunger and exposure to severe weather, Crook decided to strike out for the Black Hills for supplies and to relieve the settlements that might be threatened by the Sioux and their allies. He marched south along the divide between the waters of the Heart, Cannonball, and Grand rivers, which was a hazardous route intersected by a large number of trails toward the Black Hills, meaning the soldiers could be attacked at any time.

Describing what became known as the "Horsemeat March," an *Army & Navy Journal* correspondent reported: "Water and wood were neither plentiful nor convenient, and owing to cold rainstorms which prevailed constantly, camp life on half rations, and with no tents and little bedding, was extremely severe upon the men. Grass was abundant; nevertheless a number of animals had to be dropped, and the march was a severe strain on the entire column" (*ANJ*, September 23, 1876: 101).

OPPOSITE
Capt. Frederick Van Vliet and other officers of the 3d Cavalry pose for the camera of Stanley J. Morrow near Custer City, Black Hills, Dakota Territory, after their action at Slim Buttes. (Denver Public Library Western Collection X-31735)

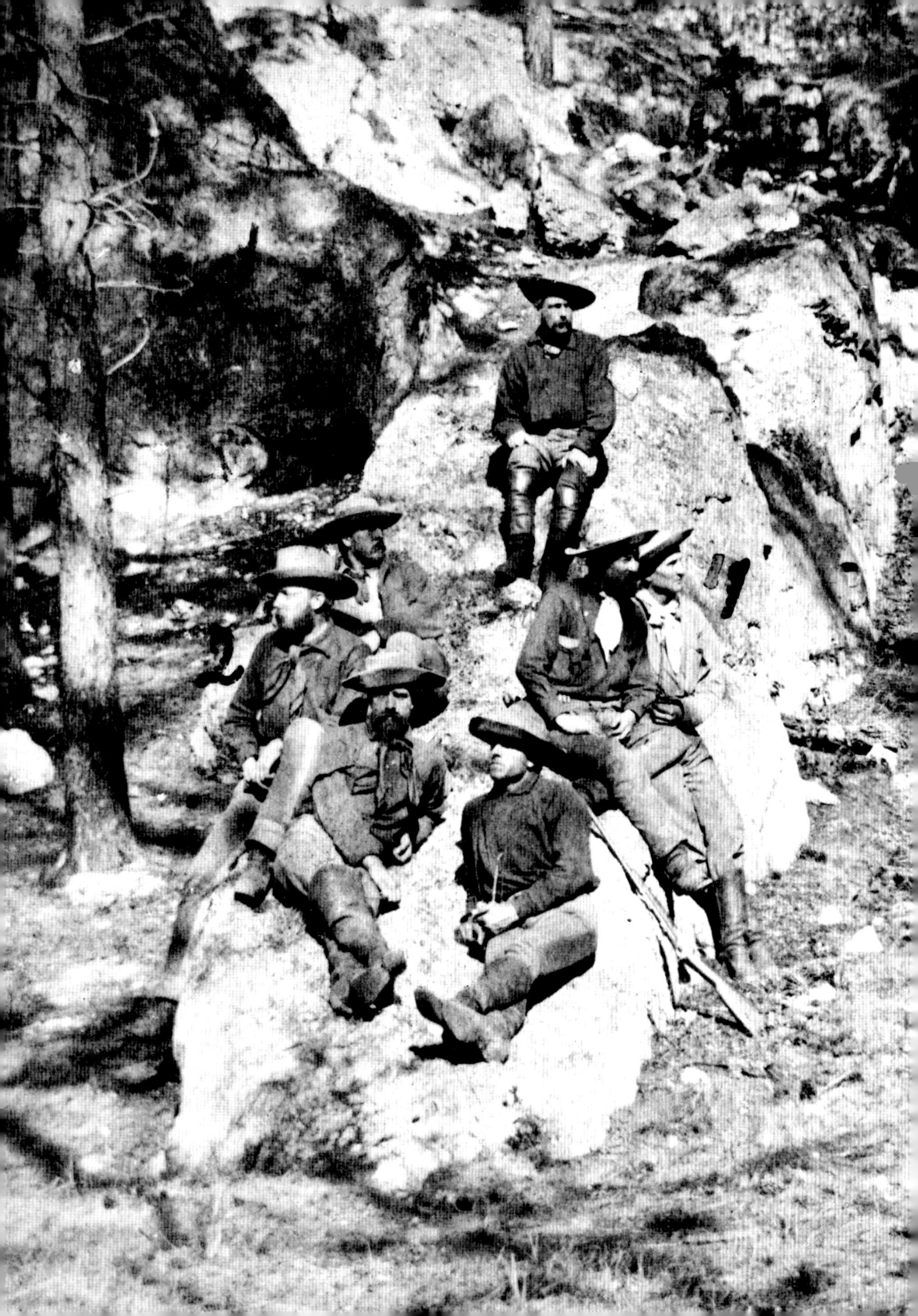

Slim Buttes, September 8–10, 1876

MAP KEY

1 *c.*1500hrs, September 8: Scout Frank Grouard discovers a Sioux encampment about a half-mile to the east of Slim Buttes.

2 0200hrs, September 9: Mills is detached with a small command and marches toward the encampment.

3 *c.*0230–0400hrs, September 9: Mills leaves the pack train and approaches the encampment in three parallel columns, the outer two being dismounted, and the center one mounted.

4 *c.*0430hrs, September 9: The Native American pony herd is spooked by the approach of the two dismounted columns and stampedes through the encampment, waking the Native Americans.

5 *c.*0430–0500hrs, September 9: Schwatka's mounted detachment charges through the village, and the dismounted troopers open fire. Many of the Native Americans manage to escape. Some seek refuge in a ravine on the south side of the creek, while others ride off to warn Crazy Horse who is camped farther south.

6 *c.*0500hrs, September 9: Mills sends couriers for reinforcement from Crook.

7 *c.*0500hrs, September 9: Some of the warriors stand their ground and open fire, and Mills' troopers entrench and await reinforcements.

8 *c.*1000–1400hrs, September 9: Crook's column arrives on the battlefield.

9 *c.*1030–1400hrs, September 9: Crook's force bivouacs and the captured village is burnt.

10 *c.*1400hrs, September 9: American Horse surrenders Native American women and children hiding in ravine.

11 *c.*1615hrs, September 9: Warriors led by Crazy Horse attack Crook's bivouacked force.

12 *c.*1615–1715hrs, September 9: Dismounted cavalry, and infantry, are ordered to advance south and west at the run in skirmish order. Mounted elements of the 2d Cavalry form on the eastern flank of the encampment and the 9th Infantry guards its northern approaches. The irregular perimeter thus formed foils the main thrust of the attack and the Native Americans withdraw at dusk.

13 *c.*0600hrs, September 10: Crook's column marches southwest toward Crook City in the Black Hills for supplies. The Native Americans attack his cavalry rearguard which is formed by dismounted skirmish order.

Battlefield environment

The Sioux called Slim Buttes "Paha Zizipela," which means thin butte and was a reference to the whole range of buttes which ran from north to south for about 50 miles in northwestern Dakota Territory. The site of the battlefield lay in open rolling prairie about 3 miles east of the main range of buttes, which ran around it in a rough semicircle. About a half-mile to the southwest of the Native American encampment stood three small steep-walled, flat-topped buttes rising to about 50–75ft above the plain, beyond which more buttes formed deep canyons and stood in much more broken terrain. The Native American encampment was situated on either side of Gap Creek, which flowed in an easterly direction.

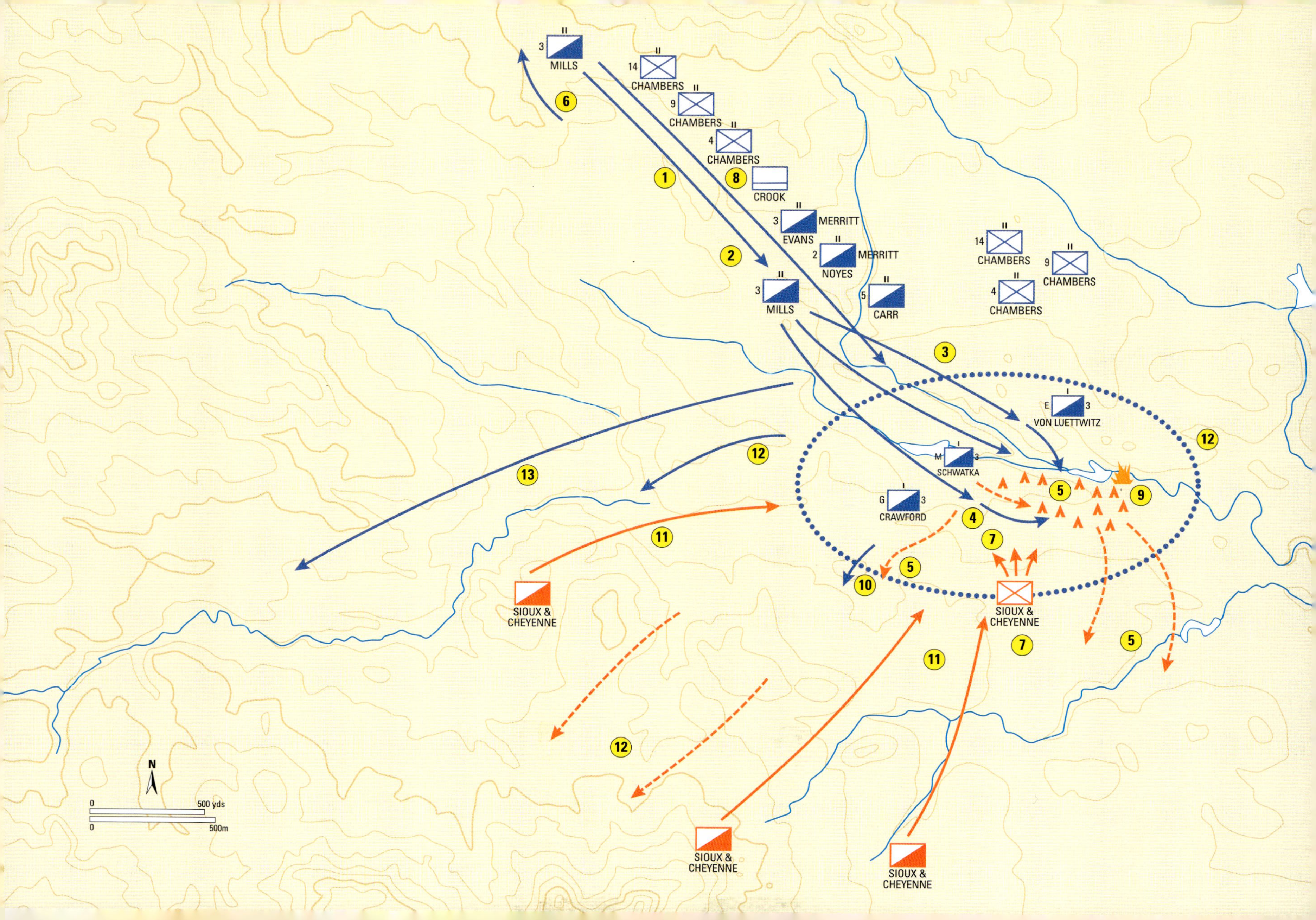

MILLS
CHAMBERS
CHAMBERS
CHAMBERS
CROOK
EVANS
MERRITT
NOYES
MERRITT
MILLS
CARR
CHAMBERS
CHAMBERS
CHAMBERS
VON LUETTWITZ
SCHWATKA
CRAWFORD
SIOUX & CHEYENNE
SIOUX & CHEYENNE
SIOUX & CHEYENNE
SIOUX & CHEYENNE
N
0
500 yds
0
500m

INTO COMBAT

On September 7, Crook sent a portion of his pack train ahead to get much-needed supplies from Deadwood City, in the Black Hills, under escort of 150 men commanded by Capt. Anson Mills, with 15 men on the best horses of each company of the 3d Cavalry. Subordinate officers consisted of 1/Lt. Adolphus H. Von Luettwitz (Co. E), 2/Lt. Frederick G. Schwatka (Co. M), and 1/Lt. Emmett Crawford (Co. G), with chief of commissary 1/Lt. John W. Bubb (Co. I), 4th Infantry. Crook's chief scout Frank Grouard guided the party, aided by "Captain Jack" Crawford, with Thomas Moore as chief packer. Significantly, if Mills encountered a Native American village on his march he was instructed to "lose no opportunity" to strike it (*DIO*, October 4, 1876: 1:6).

At about 1500hrs on September 8, Grouard discovered through the rain and fog, without being observed himself, a Sioux encampment about a half-mile to the east of Slim Buttes, which was later learned to be of the bands of American Horse and Roman Nose who were supposedly on their way back into the Cheyenne Agency. The village consisted of 37 lodges and a herd of several hundred ponies, plus a few captured American horses. Deciding he would attempt an attack without waiting for reinforcements, Mills fell back several miles and hid his command in a ravine. Accompanying the expedition, a correspondent for the *Philadelphia Inquirer* wrote: "We marched back 2 miles and bivouacked in a pocket formed by two canyons in the deep mud, and drenched with battering rain" (*PI*, September 18, 1876: 1:4). In his official report Mills wrote: "The night was one of the ugliest I ever passed, dark, cold, rainy, and muddy in the extreme" (*DIO*, October 4, 1876: 2:6).

At 0200hrs next morning, Mills marched his small command toward the encampment. When within 1 mile of it, Mills left the pack train consisting of 125 animals, with 25 men to hold them, under the command of Bubb. Approaching the village before daylight, his plan of attack involved three parallel columns of troops, the outer two being dismounted, and the center one mounted. The column on the right, numbering 57 men, was under Crawford, while that on the left, numbering 53 men was under Von Luettwitz. Commanded by Schwatka, the 25 mounted men in the center column were to wait for their dismounted comrades to silently surround the encampment in skirmish order and, on command of a bugle call, charge through the village driving the Native American ponies before them. As the Native Americans attempted to escape the dismounted men would open fire, and be joined by Schwatka's troopers who would turn and fire having reached the other side of the village, thus creating a lethal crossfire.

The two dismounted columns advanced cautiously until they were within 100yd of the Native American pony herd when the animals were spooked and, according to the *Philadelphia Inquirer* reporter, "rushed like a hurricane toward the village" (*PI*, September 18, 1876: 1:4). Of these events Mills, who was with Von Luettwitz's detachment, wrote:

> Gruard [sic] then informed me that the chance for a total surprise was entirely lost … I ordered the charge sounded, and right gallantly did Schwatka … execute it. Immediately the dismounted detachment charged on the south side, and

commenced firing at the Indians, who, finding themselves laced in their lodges, the leather drawn tight as a drum by the rain, had quickly cut themselves out with their knives and returned our fire, the squaws carrying off the dead, wounded, and children up the opposite bluff, leaving everything … in our possession. (*DIO*, October 4, 1876: 2:6)

Red Horse, who was sleeping in one of the lodges when the attack began, recalled: "It was early morning, still dark and misting. We were all asleep. The first we knew we were fired upon, we caught up what arms we could find in the dark, the women taking the children and hiding among the rocks … Seven of my people were killed and four wounded at that time. Some of my horses were shot. The troops captured all our lodges, all our buffalo robes, and we had a great many. They took all we had" (Sioux War Papers, National Archives). Also in the camp, 17-year-old Charger recollected:

> Troops of cavalry ran into the camp while the Indians were yet sleeping, and commenced to fire into them. The Indians fled naked, some of their ponies stampeded and all of the ponies were taken by the soldiers, except a few which ran in the direction of the fleeing Indians were not taken. As some of these ponies were caught by the Indians some rode double on their ponies and made their escape. All their tents, food, and other articles such as beadwork were destroyed by fire, leaving some of the fleeing Indians almost helpless, and in a destitute condition. (Charger 1928: 308)

Photographed by Stanley J. Morrow after the capture of the Slim Buttes village on September 8, 1876, a guidon taken from Custer's battalion on Last Stand Hill rests against a Native American lodge and represents revenge for the massacre at the Little Bighorn. Standing left to right: scout Frank Grouard; Sgt. Ferdinand Culbertson; and 2/Lt. Frederick G. Schwatka. Sitting from left to right: Lt. Col. William B. Royall; Capt. William H. Andrews; Capt. Anson Mills; and 1/Lt. Joseph Lawson. (Denver Public Library Western Collection X-31736)

As soon as the warriors had got their women and children to relative safety in a ravine across the creek, they turned on their assailants and opened fire on the cavalrymen, who began to entrench. During the heat of the action, Grouard reported to Mills that some of the Native Americans were escaping and, based on tracks discovered, there were other villages nearby. Fearing another Custer-style massacre, Mills sent the scout to the rear with orders to dispatch a courier to Crook immediately, requesting reinforcements. Observing this incident, the *Philadelphia Inquirer* reporter recalled:

> Two men volunteered for this service and galloped off … We then advanced into the valley under fire. The fusillade was continuous, and bullets came whizzing from nearly every acclivity. A low ridge hid the village from view, and at its foot were herded two hundred captured ponies. Gaining the ridge the fire upon us became nearer for a time, but well restrained by our skirmishers commanding the village. (*PI*, September 18, 1876: 1:4)

According to Charger, the warrior Burnt Thigh relayed developments to the main Native American camp. Red Horse, riding with those who managed to escape, recalled: "We gathered up a few horses and put our families on them and went to the main camp [on the southwest side of Slim Buttes] … where we told what had happened. A large body of young men went out in pursuit … We were coming in here to stay – to give ourselves up [at the Cheyenne Agency] … when we were attacked" (Sioux War Papers, National Archives). Although not present during this fight, Many Shields related, "About two thousand warriors started in pursuit" (Buell 1876).

Meanwhile at the American Horse encampment, Mills' troopers started coming under heavy fire as the Native Americans rallied, and he later reported "as my command was almost entirely engaged with the wounded, the held horses, and the skirmish line, I determined to leave the collection of the property and provisions with which the village was supplied to the main command on its arrival" (*DIO*, October 4, 1876: 2:6).

The 5th Cavalry was the first to reach the battleground about 1000hrs followed by the battalions of the 2d and 3d Cavalry, the pack train, and the battalions of infantry. By 1400hrs Crook had his whole force assembled. About 100yd from the encampment was a ravine in which a band of seven warriors, including American Horse, and 15 women and children hid in a cavern of rocks. It was while attempting to dislodge them that Crook sustained one killed and three wounded. In an effort to save the women and children, Crook eventually parleyed with the Native Americans through Frank Grouard and, as a result, three warriors surrendered, including a mortally wounded American Horse. Thus the lives of some of the Native American women and children were saved.

Going into bivouac, Crook's command was spread around the scene of the morning action. The cavalry rested for over a half-mile along the ridge immediately northwest of the village and parallel with Gap Creek. The infantry were camped farther north around the field hospital. The horses were staked out on the swales and ridges to the north and south of the creek. Meanwhile, Co. G, 4th Infantry, burned and destroyed the village.

At about 1615hrs the Sioux under Crazy Horse began to arrive in numbers from the southwest, attacking the pickets of the 5th Cavalry and wounding three men. The afternoon action had commenced. One of the 700 or so braves who responded to the attack, the Northern Cheyenne Tall Bull commented briefly in later years, "Some [of the survivors] ran to us and we attacked the soldiers and fought most of the day" (Camp Interview Notes). According to Crook's *aide-de-camp* Lt. Walter S. Schuyler, there was a rush when the enemy approached in force. The alarm was given just in time, as the Sioux were well mounted compared to the worn-out Army horses (Schmidt 1946: 207).

After attempting unsuccessfully to drive off the cavalry horses, most of the warriors withdrew and occupied the bluffs south of the village. Crook immediately deployed his troops in skirmish order around the encampment, and a combined force of dismounted cavalrymen, consisting of elements of the 2d, 3d, and 5th Cavalry, and infantrymen, composed of companies of the 4th, 9th, and 14th Infantry, advanced south and west "at the run" and pushing the Native Americans back into the bluffs and beyond. At the same time mounted elements of the 2d Cavalry guarded the eastern flank, and two companies of the 9th Infantry protected the northern approaches.

Among the Sioux captured at Slim Buttes was Charging Bear, standing at center, and his wives and children. These Native Americans were captured with American Horse and Charging Bear was dragged out of the ravine with only one cartridge left. He later became the chief spokesman for the Native Americans at the Standing Rock Agency. (Denver Public Library Western Collection X-31748)

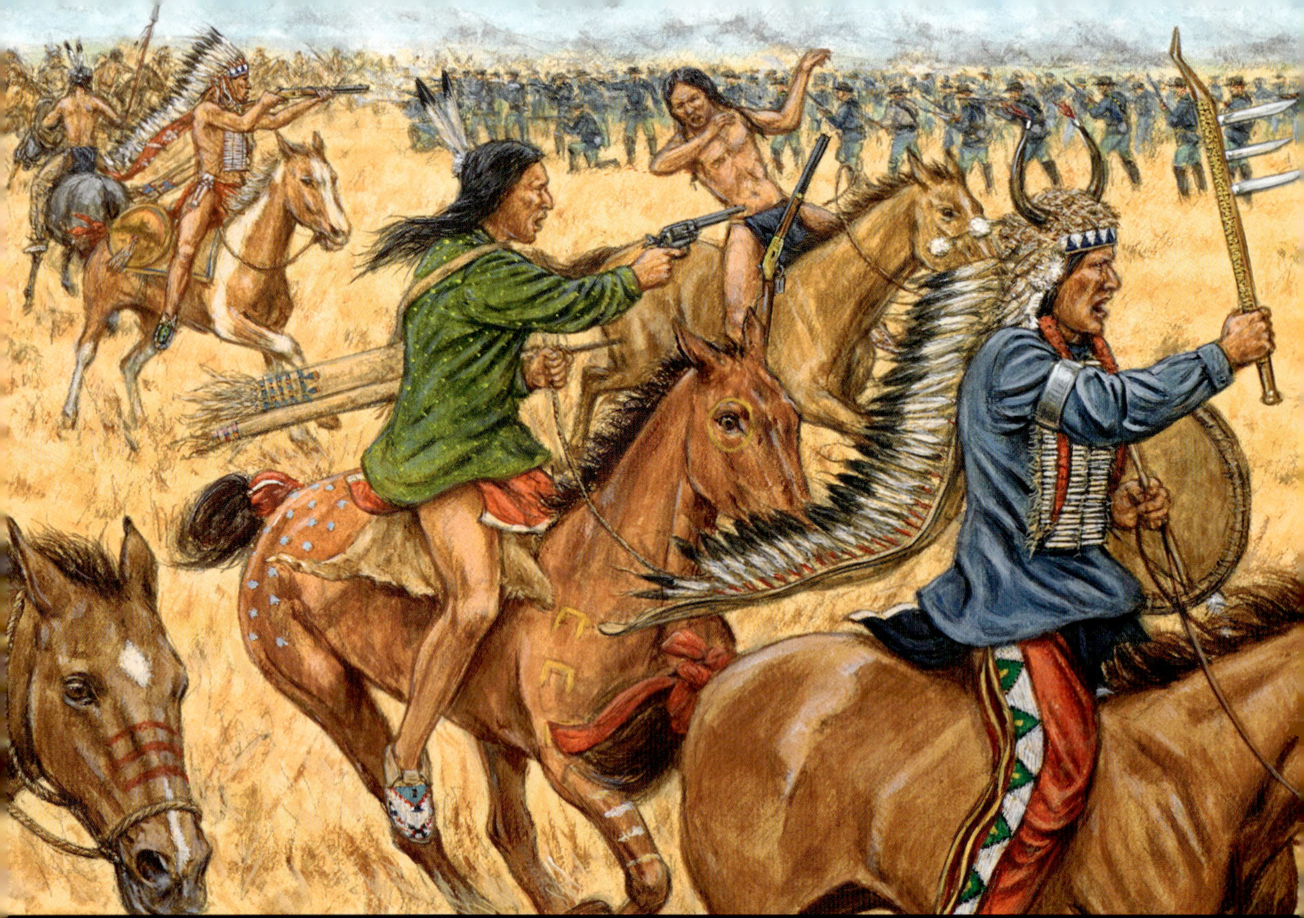

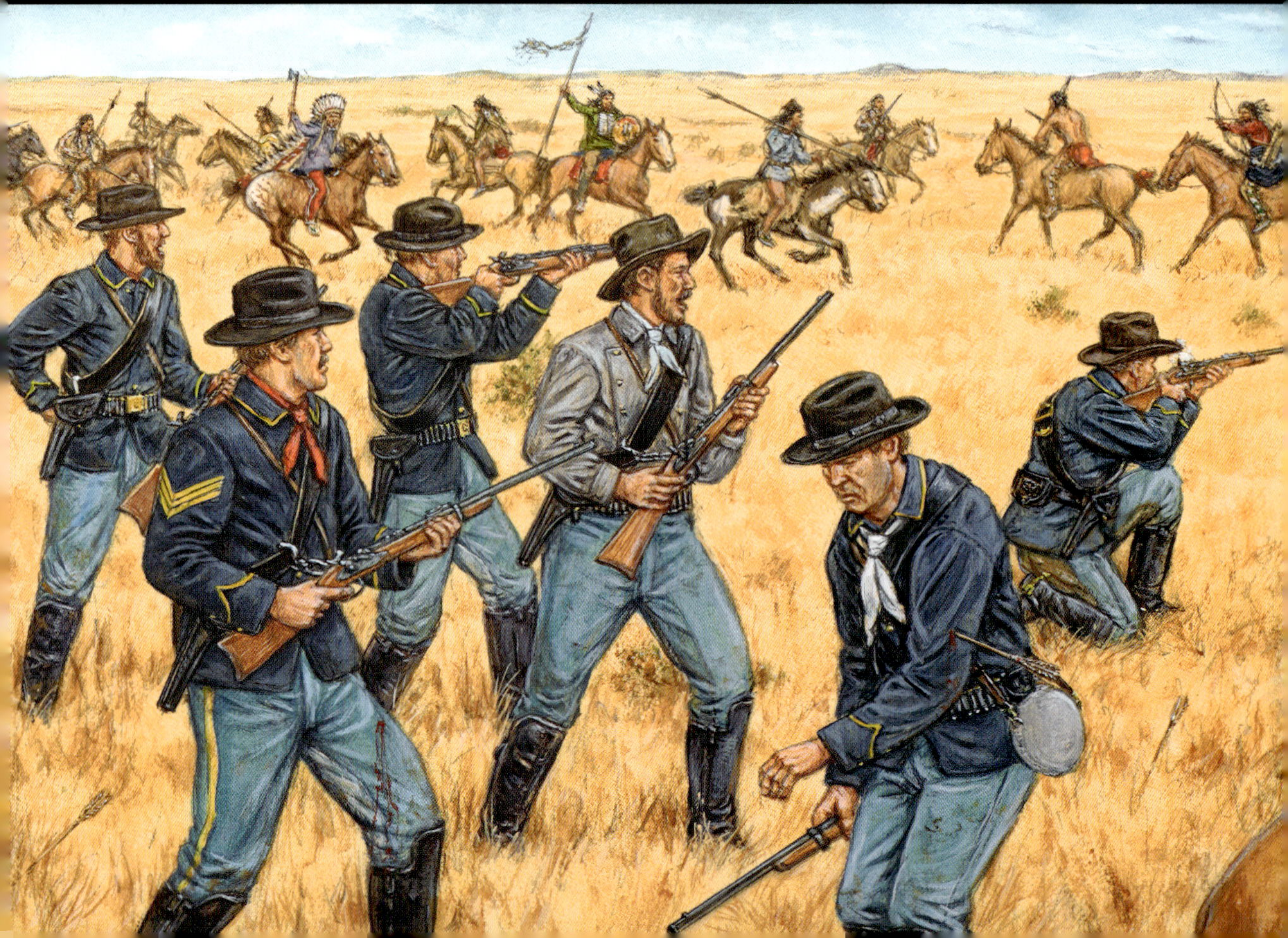

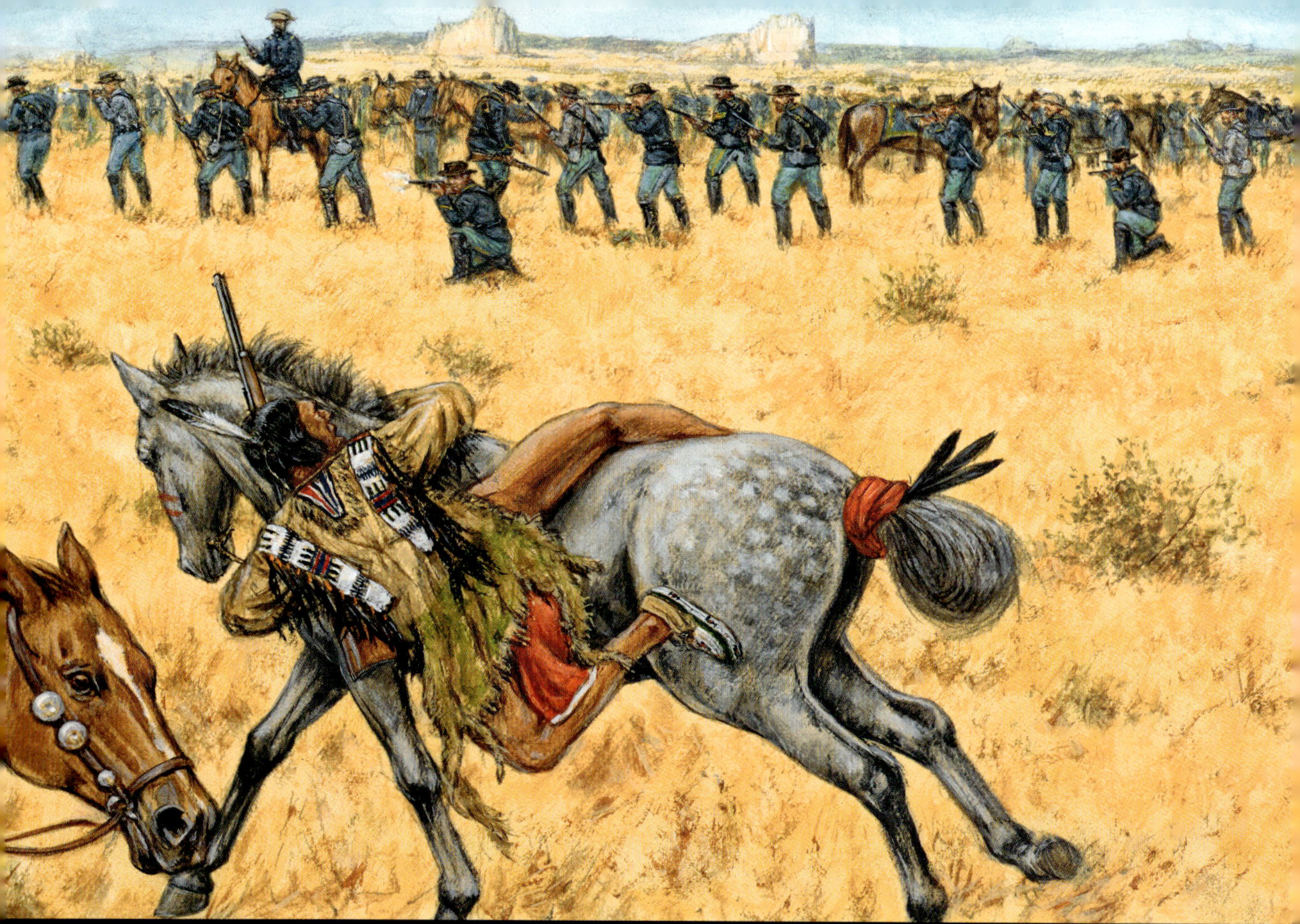

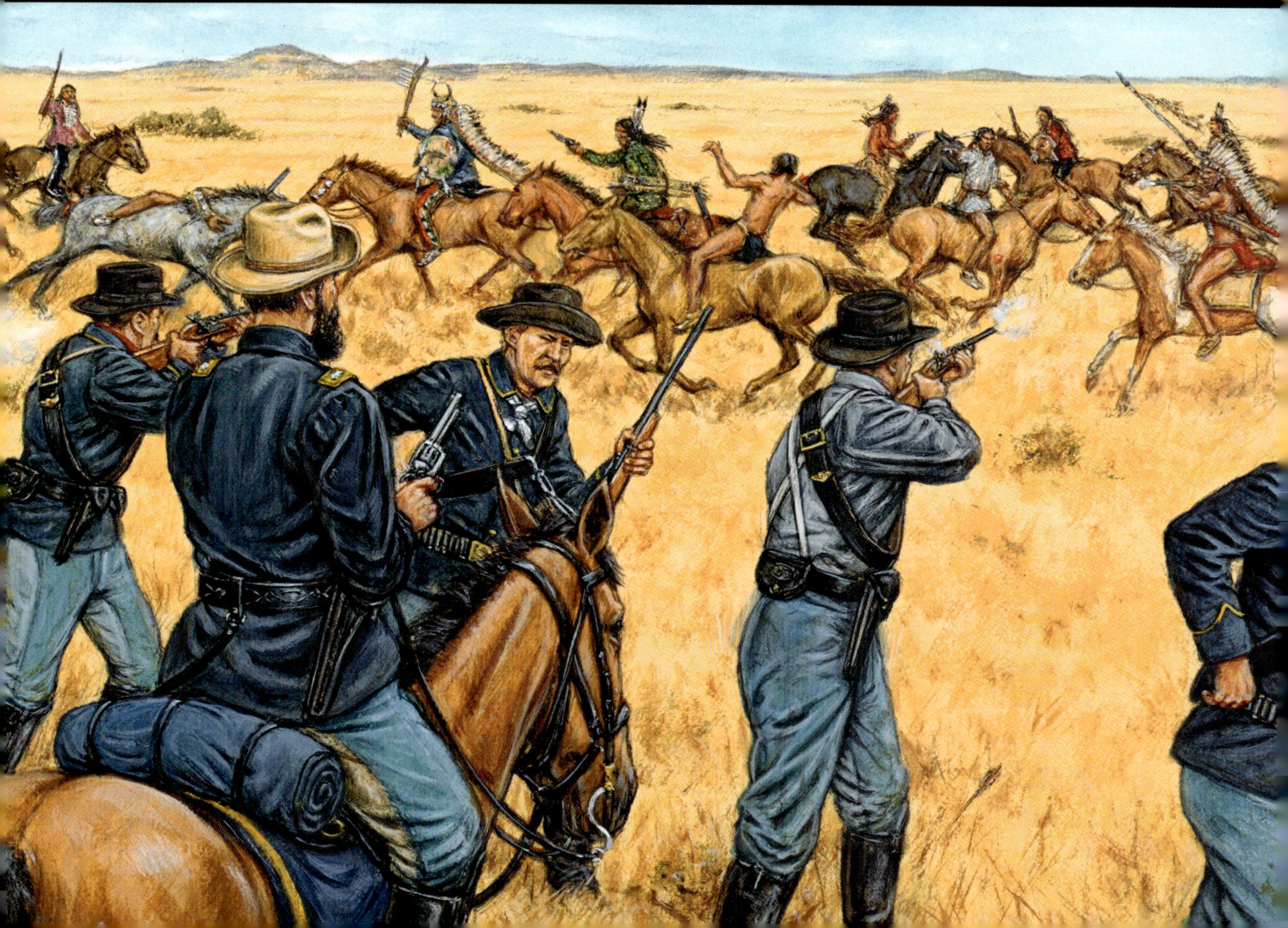

"The most beautiful Indian combat..."

Native American view: Sioux warriors led by Crazy Horse attack elements of the "great, irregular circle" formed by US cavalry and infantry of the Big Horn and Yellowstone Expedition under Brig. Gen. George R. Crook at Slim Buttes on September 9, 1876 (*DIO*, October 4, 1876: 2:5). Many of these Native Americans were involved in the defeat and massacre of Custer and the 7th Cavalry at the Little Bighorn. They are desperate to recover their ponies, capture the worn-out US cavalry horses, and free the Native Americans taken prisoner by Capt. Anson Mills earlier that day. Mounted on fleet ponies, a group of braves defy the carbine gunfire, attempting to probe and find a weak point in Crook's lines. Urging the warriors forward, He Dog wears a trailer war bonnet and beaded war shirt, and brandishes a studded knife club and shield. With a Model 1873 Winchester repeating rifle in hand, another prominent Sioux leader called Kicking Bear leans behind his galloping pony to avoid the flying bullets. In his eagerness for revenge, a young warrior ventures ahead of the others and is knocked off his pony by a well-aimed shot from a trooper in the long blue line. The smoke from the burning lodges of American Horse billows in the background.

US cavalry view: Troopers of the 5th Cavalry deploy in dismounted skirmish order to drive off the Sioux warriors massing on the bluffs and flats around them. With drawn Colt revolver, Lt. Col. Eugene A. Carr, commanding the cavalry brigade, sits his mount unmoved as bullets whistle by him. Sergeant Lucifer Schreiber of Co. K is struck by a bullet in the thigh as he stands composedly watching his men as they blaze away with their Springfield carbines. Another trooper limps away from the line having been struck in the arm by a well-aimed arrow. Stepping a few yards ahead of the line, Pvt. "Paddy" Nihil, of Co. F, kneels, takes aim, and tumbles a Native American off his pony, and several other troopers nearby cheer at his successful shooting. Regarding the afternoon action at Slim Buttes on September 9, 1/Lt. Charles King, Co. K, 5th Cavalry, recalled it was "the most beautiful Indian combat" he had ever seen, "for there were thousands engaged on the two sides" (*ES*, April 13, 1889: 10:2).

Of the unfolding action, 1/Lt. Charles King, Co. K, 5th Cavalry, wrote:

> On four sides of ... a great, irregular circle, the combat is at its height. First in one place, then in another, by furious dashes the Indians strive to break the lines, but everywhere are met by cool, steady volleys. "Halt" and "lie down" have long since been signaled and the skirmishers are now prone upon the sward, for the Indians have been pushed so far back that their bullets no longer endanger the herds and the wounded in the village. Little by little the fire slackens; little by little the dripping skies change from gray to dun, then to brownish blue, then night settles down on crag and prairie; the red flashes grow less and less frequent, and at last die utterly away. Slowly the lines were drawn in while strong picket guards are posted, slowly and tenderly the seriously wounded men are borne back to the surgeon's lodges. The adjutants tramp around from battalion to battalion making up the list of casualties ... (*DIO*, April 27, 1889: 20:2)

Following the previous day of fighting, Crook made no further effort to pursue, but concentrated on getting his command back to a regular supply source. Of the second day of action, King wrote: "Morning of September 10 broke wet, raw, and cold. A mist hovered over the surface of the earth and wisps of cloud floated across the face and summits of the buttes ... Well out on the slopes, crouching behind their improvised rifle pits ... pickets could be seen wearily watching for the first appearance of the Sioux" (*CL*, May 5, 1889: 13:4).

Crook buried his two dead with "scant ceremony" and, as his column departed, ordered it to march directly over the graves to destroy their location and prevent the Sioux from digging up the corpses and disfiguring them. King recalled:

> No sooner did it become apparent to the Indians, crowding all around us on the heights, that Crook's army was marching away than down they came at the burning village. They paid no attention to the long columns crawling snake-like away to the south – the pack trains with their guards, the cavalry and infantry skirmishers thrown well out on both sides and marching "by the flank." With one accord they came swooping down from north and west, yelling rage and defiance, and blazing away at the long lines of cavalry skirmishers, dismounted to stand them off. (*CL*, May 5, 1889: 13:4)

On September 13, Crook finally obtained supplies from Crook City in the Black Hills, which ended the ordeal of his men. Of the movements of the Native Americans at the end of the second day of fighting, Red Horse commented: "The main body then left Slim Buttes and traveled to the Yellowstone where they camped below the mouth of the Tongue river" (Sioux War Papers, National Archives).

Army casualties at Slim Buttes on September 9–10, 1876 numbered two troopers and one scout killed and 23 troopers wounded. Two enlisted men of Co. M, 3d Cavalry, were awarded Medals of Honor for bravery. Due to their custom of carrying their dead and wounded off the battlefield, it is impossible to determine how many Native American casualties there were, although news correspondent Finerty claimed that approximately ten Native Americans were killed or wounded (Finerty 1890: 342–43).

Analysis

THE ROSEBUD

Compared with previous actions in frontier warfare, the battle at the Rosebud was a long and bloody fight. Never before had the Plains Indians fought with such ferocity. Neither had they been prepared to receive such high casualties in battle, but they were fighting to defend their families and nomadic lifestyle.

The lack of any spectacular success in the Yellowstone Expedition prior to the Rosebud rankled deeply with Brig. Gen. Crook, and the action on June 17, 1876, was the only major setback he had suffered in 20 years of campaigning against Native Americans. In his official report he stated that he was operating in very rough and broken terrain in which his column was attacked on all sides. This, he claimed, forced him to divide his command in order to meet attacks from all sides. He further maintained that such an action would have been indecisive unless he captured the Sioux village which he believed was close by (Vaughn 1956: 195–96). Nevertheless, he was ultimately responsible for the fact that elements of his cavalry were lured out of support range causing his cavalry to become fragmented while trying to destroy a very mobile enemy.

Furthermore, the Rosebud was a strategic defeat for Crook as it prevented his immediate junction with Brig. Gen. Terry's command, an event which would most likely have produced a different beginning, and doubtless a successful end, to what happened at the Little Bighorn eight days later. For years after, a dispute raged between Crook and Lt. Col. Royall, his cavalry commander, as to the reasons for their lack of success at the Rosebud. Royall accused Crook of poor battlefield performance, while Crook responded that Royall's reluctance to rejoin him immediately after being ordered back from his isolated position near Kollmar Creek cost them dearly. Crook further claimed that the opportunity to launch a cavalry charge was missed because Royall took nearly three hours to carry out orders to rejoin the main force (Schmidt 1946: 195–96).

ABOVE LEFT
The remains of Custer and his officers were buried at Fort Leavenworth on August 4, 1876. This engraving from a sketch by J. Howell was published in *Frank Leslie's Illustrated Newspaper* on September 8, 1877. At the conclusion of the burial services, the guard of honor fired a salute of three volleys, each loaded with ball cartridges rather than blanks, as a sign they would avenge the death of their fallen comrades. (Author's collection)

ABOVE RIGHT
Crow scouts (left to right) Hairy Moccasin, White Man Runs Him, Curly, and Goes Ahead visit Custer's death-site marker in 1908. (Little Bighorn Battlefield National Monument LIBI 00019 00435)

In the aftermath of the Rosebud, an unidentified participant in the battle admitted that the Army had underestimated the fighting capabilities of the Sioux and Cheyenne, stating that "the mere shaking of a buffalo robe, as some officers have claimed, will not make them run. They are quick to seize positions, quick to give them up when necessary to seize better ones; are far better armed than our troopers, and in fact possess all possible elements necessary to make the best light troopers in the world" (quoted in *ANJ*, July 22, 1876: 801–02).

THE LITTLE BIGHORN

The annihilation of Lt. Col. Custer's battalion at the Little Bighorn left the US Army, and indeed the American nation, in a state of shock. When his column reached the scene of devastation on Last Stand Hill and he found Custer's remains, Terry is reported to have said tearfully, "The flower of the army is gone at last" (*NYH*, July 14, 1876: 5:6). A few days later Terry wrote Crook that he was "astounded at the number and skill of the enemy," and commented that the situation was "'scarey' [*sic*] in the extreme," but denied there was any "insecure feeling among the soldiers" (*ANJ*, August 5, 1876: 837).

At the Little Bighorn, Custer brought about his own demise, plus that of 272 other officers, enlisted men, scouts, civilians, and auxiliaries, by taking on virtually the whole Sioux nation, and its allies, with a single regiment, even if it was the 7th Cavalry. His refusal to sacrifice the speed and mobility of his mounted column by the inclusion of the lumbering Gatling gun battery offered by Terry is understandable, but such deadly weaponry would probably have made the difference on the day.

Custer had been a risk-taking soldier earlier in his career in both the Civil War (1861–65) and the Indian Wars. He also had possible political aspirations and hoped that further success on the battlefield would be a springboard to a successful candidacy. In his typically audacious style, he may have had designs on being president someday, and victory over the Sioux and their allies would have done much to pave his way to the White House. However, the events which unfolded on the windswept bluffs above the Little Bighorn on June 25, 1876, militated against that.

The exhausted condition of some of Custer's cavalrymen and their mounts played a significant role in the disaster. A few weeks after the battle, Capt. Benteen wrote: "on the 22d [June], the cavalry marched twelve miles; on the 23rd, twenty-five miles; from 5 a.m. till 8 p.m., of the 24th, forty-five miles, and then after night ten miles further, resting, but without unsaddling, twenty-three miles, to the battle-field" (*ANJ*, July 15, 1876: 791). Once engaged in the fighting, Custer divided his already depleted regiment into three small battalions, and fought an enemy of vastly superior numbers and firepower on unfamiliar ground. Even the unshakable self-belief of Custer, and the faith he had in the invincibility of the 7th Cavalry, could not overcome such odds.

According to the Cheyenne warrior Young Two Moon, "If these soldiers had all stood together the Indians could have done nothing with them" (Grinnell Collection). As Custer approached the Native American encampment, the Crow scout Half Yellow Face had objected to his tactics, stating through interpreter and scout "Mitch" Boyer that there were too many of the enemy and that Custer should keep his command all together. Custer brushed off the scout's warning and Half Yellow Face started to strip off his soldier clothing and paint his face for battle (Lehman 2010: 99).

Certainly, Custer was let down by Maj. Reno and Benteen, who did not come to his aid when needed. As a result of the court of inquiry at Chicago in 1879, Reno was exonerated from charges of drinking and cowardice in the face of the enemy at the Little Bighorn. This did little to change public opinion, however, and enlisted men who testified later stated they had been coerced into giving a positive report to Reno. During the same year, while commanding officer at Fort Meade, Dakota Territory, Reno again faced court-martial, charged with conduct unbecoming an officer because of his drinking. This time he was convicted and dismissed from the service on April 1, 1880. In 1904, a report in the *Northwestern Christian Advocate* claimed that Reno had admitted to its former editor that "his strange actions" at the Little Bighorn were "due to drink" (*NCA*, September 7, 1904: 3).

At the same court of inquiry, Benteen explained that if he had carried out Custer's order to advance with the ammunition packs, his three companies would possibly have been hacked to pieces en route to Last Stand Hill. He added this would have left Reno's battalion weakened, and when Terry's column arrived he would have found every single man of the 7th Cavalry dead. Of the Sioux, Benteen would later state, "We were at their hearths and homes. Their medicine was working well, and they were fighting for all the good God gives anyone to fight for" (quoted in Brininstool 1933: 32).

When interviewed over a year after the battle, Sitting Bull commented, "These men who came with the Long Hair were as good men as fought. When they rode up their horses were tired and they were tired. When they got off from their horses they could not stand firmly on their feet. They swayed to and fro – so my young men have told me – like the limbs of cypresses in a great wind" (*NYH*, November 16, 1877: 4:1).

SLIM BUTTES

The attack on the encampment at Slim Buttes was an act of revenge for the Little Bighorn disaster and salvaged something from the summer campaign of 1876. Having captured the village of American Horse, who had participated in the action on Last Stand Hill, the cavalry under Crook's command searched the Native American lodges and found a guidon carried by Co. I of the 7th Cavalry, a pair of gloves marked "Colonel Keogh," and parts of other officers' and non-commissioned officers' uniforms, plus several troopers' saddles, while horses in the herd bore the mark of the regiment. An abundance of dried meat also meant their "starvation march" was over (*PI*, September 18, 1876: 1:4–5; *DIO*, October 4, 1876: 2:6).

However, the significant effect of Slim Buttes was not so much to inflict maximum punishment on the Native Americans, nor to pursue a policy of "total war" or extermination, as the Native Americans probably suffered fewer than a dozen casualties during the action. It was more a blow to their morale due to the significant loss and destruction of property.

In his own analysis of the campaign leading to the attack, Crook attributed the problems he experienced first to not having enough mules for transport, which led to the "starvation march," and second to the lack of Native American auxiliaries and scouts. Disgusted with the poor result of the summer campaign, the Utes and Shoshones had left Crook's command on August 20. This limited his reconnaissance capability to the extent that any positive results in finding the Sioux and their allies were a matter of luck. Nevertheless, the battle at Slim Buttes set the pattern for the relentless pursuit of the Native Americans and the destruction of their supplies which followed during the next 14 years, and some of the Sioux called it "The Fight Where We Lost the Black Hills" (Bray 2006: 245).

A detail from one of Stanley J. Morrow's "Views of Gen. Crook's Expedition and the Black Hills" shows a wounded soldier being carried on a mule litter after the fight at Slim Buttes. On the second day at Slim Buttes the circle formed by Crook's force kept the warriors of Crazy Horse at bay, and Army commanders seem to have learned that flanking attacks requiring the splitting up of larger commands into smaller units of men was not the way to defeat the highly mobile Sioux and Cheyenne. (Library of Congress LC-DIG-stereo-1s00439)

Aftermath

Many of the Sioux and their allies returned to the reservations following the battles of 1876, and the number of warriors still in the field was reduced to about 600. During the fall of that year, Col. Nelson A. Miles met with Sitting Bull near Cedar Creek in Montana Territory but failed to persuade him to surrender. After Slim Buttes, the Army continued to seek out the remaining Native American encampments. Further significant actions occurred on November 25, 1876, at the Dull Knife Fight, and on January 8, 1877, with Crazy Horse at Wolf Mountain. On May 5, 1877, Sitting Bull led the remainder of his warriors and their families across the border into Canada. The next day, Crazy Horse surrendered at the Red Cloud Agency, near Camp Robinson, Nebraska, where on September 5 he was killed during a struggle with a guard.

The only survivor of the fighting during the closing stages at the Little Bighorn, the mixed-breed bay gelding "Comanche" ridden by Capt. Myles W. Keogh was found badly wounded by soldiers two days after the battle. After being transported to Fort Lincoln, he was slowly nursed back to health, and after a lengthy convalescence, was retired. Thereafter, on all ceremonial occasions of mounted regimental formation, he was saddled, bridled, and draped in mourning, and led by a mounted trooper of Co. I during regimental parades. (Little Bighorn Battlefield National Monument LIBI 00019 00219)

Photographed c.1876, Crow scout Curly became a celebrated survivor of the battle of the Little Bighorn, although his claims to have witnessed the last stages of Custer's fight on "Last Stand Hill" are untrue as he probably slipped away before Custer reached the bluff at 3,411ft. Wrapping himself in a Sioux blanket, Curly is believed to have passed unnoticed through the victorious warriors and rode north to the mouth of the Little Bighorn to inform Terry's command of Custer's probable demise. Note the photographer David F. Barry's blind stamp on the image. (Little Bighorn Battlefield National Monument LIBI 00019 00190)

The Great Sioux War ended at Little Muddy Creek in Montana Territory on May 7, 1877 with Miles' defeat of a remaining band of Miniconjou Sioux led by Lame Deer. Hunger and desperation eventually forced Sitting Bull and 186 of his people to return to the United States and surrender on July 19, 1881. Ownership of the Black Hills was determined by an ultimatum issued by the Manypenny Commission of February 28, 1877, according to which the Native Americans were required to cede the land to the US in return for the continued supply of rations to the reservations. Threatened with forced starvation, they ceded the land to the United States but never accepted the legitimacy of the transaction.

ORDERS OF BATTLE

The Rosebud, June 17, 1876

Sioux and Cheyenne forces
Crazy Horse and c.1,000 warriors consisting of Oglala, Miniconjou, Sans Arc, Brule, and Hunkpapa Sioux, plus Northern Cheyenne. Casualties: c.16 KIA, 400 WIA.

Crook's Column (Big Horn and Yellowstone Expedition)
Brig. Gen. George R. Crook, plus two *aides-de-camp*, one engineer officer, one quartermaster, one assistant quartermaster, one commissary of subsistence, one chief surgeon, one chief of transportation, and one chief of scouts.

Cavalry battalions (Lt. Col. William B. Royall, plus one adjutant, one acting assistant quartermaster, one assistant surgeon, and one acting assistant surgeon):
3d Cavalry (Maj. Andrew W. Evans, plus one battalion adjutant, 20 company-grade officers, and 517 men. Casualties: 9 KIA, 15 WIA = 24).
First Battalion (Capt. Anson Mills): Co. A (1/Lt. Joseph Lawson, 2/Lt. Charles Morton, plus 55 men); Co. E (Capt. Alexander Sutorius, 1/Lt. Adolphus H. Von Luettwitz (temporary duty from Co. C), 2/Lt. Henry R. Lemly, plus 45 men. Casualties: 1 WIA); Co. I (Capt. William H. Andrews, 1/Lt. Albert King, 2/Lt. James E.H. Foster, plus 46 men. Casualties: 2 KIA, 6 WIA = 8); Co. M (1/Lt. August C. Paul, 2/Lt. Frederick G. Schwatka, plus 51 men. Casualties: 1 WIA).
Second Battalion (Capt. Guy V. Henry – WIA): Co. B (Capt. Charles Meinhold, 2/Lt. James F. Simpson, plus 63 men. Casualties: 1 WIA); Co. D (2/Lt. John G. Bourke, plus 42 men); Co. L (Capt. Peter D. Vroom, 2/Lt. George F. Chase, plus 53 men. Casualties: 5 KIA, 2 WIA = 7); Co. F (2/Lt. Bainbridge Reynolds, plus 52 men. Casualties: 2 KIA, 3 WIA = 5).
Two companies temporarily detached: Co. C (Capt. Frederick Van Vliet, plus 55 men); Co. G (1/Lt. Emmett Crawford, plus 55 men).
2d Cavalry Battalion (Capt. Henry E. Noyes, plus 8 company-grade officers and 273 men. Casualties: 2 WIA): Co. A (Capt. Thomas B. Dewees, 2/Lt. Daniel C. Pearson, plus 56 men); Co. B (1/Lt. William C. Rawolle, plus 60 men); Co. D (1/Lt. Samuel M. Swigert, 2/Lt. Henry D. Huntington, plus 63 men. Casualties: 1 WIA); Co. E (Capt. Elijah R. Wells, 2/Lt. Frederick W. Sibley, plus 53 men); Co. I (2/Lt. Frederick W. Kingsbury, plus 41 men. Casualties: 1 WIA).
Infantry battalion (Maj. Alexander Chambers, plus one adjutant, one acting assistant surgeon, 10 company-grade officers, and 191 men. Casualties: 3 WIA): Co. D, 4th Infantry (Capt. Avery B. Cain, 1/Lt. Henry Seton, plus 39 men. Casualties: 3 WIA); Co. F, 4th Infantry (Capt. Gerhard L. Luhn, plus 41 men); Co. C, 9th Infantry (Capt. Samuel Munson, 1/Lt. Thaddeus H. Capron, plus 46 men); Co. G, 9th Infantry (Capt. Thomas B. Burrowes, 1/Lt. William L. Carpenter, Capt. Julius H. Patski (assistant surgeon), plus 33 men); Co. H, 9th Infantry (Capt. Andrew S. Burt, 2/Lt. Edgar B. Robertson, plus 32 men).

Army scouts (Capt. George M. Randall; Frank Grouard, interpreter and scout).
Crow and Shoshone allies (total strength 262). Casualties: 1 KIA, 7 WIA = 8.
Packers (Chief of Pack Train, Thomas Moore; total strength 20).
Montana miners (total strength 65).
Wagon trains (Master, Charles Russel; 116 men).

The Little Bighorn, June 25, 1876

Sioux and Cheyenne forces
Sitting Bull and Crazy Horse, commanding c.4,000 Sioux and c.1,000 Cheyenne. Casualties: although unknown, an accurate minimum is 66 warriors, women, and children, of whom 46 were killed, plus at least 100 wounded, on Last Stand Hill.

7th Cavalry
Overall strength (as reorganized on June 25, 1876): uniformed personnel – 31 officers and 576 men = 607, plus 48 civilians and sundries = 655. Total casualties: 268 KIA, 52 WIA.

Custer's battalion
HQ: Lt. Col. George A. Custer commanding, plus one regimental adjutant, one assistant surgeon, one acting *aide-de-camp*, one sergeant major, one chief trumpeter, two trumpeters, one staff sergeant, and one hospital orderly, plus two Quartermaster Department scouts, four

Crow scouts, and two civilians. Casualties = 13 KIA. Plus ten company-grade officers and 251 men, of whom 52 were on detached duty = 275 all personnel. Casualties = 197. Total casualties on Last Stand Hill: 210 KIA.

Co. C: Capt. Thomas W. Custer, 2/Lt. Henry M. Harrington, plus 50 men. Detached: 8 men with the pack train plus 1 messenger. -5 stragglers. Casualties on Last Stand Hill: 37 KIA.

Co. I: Capt. Myles W. Keogh, 1/Lt. James E. Porter, plus 46 men. Detached: 9 men with the pack train. -1 straggler. Casualties: 38 KIA.

Co. L: 1/Lt. James Calhoun, 2/Lt. John J. Crittenden, plus 57 men. Detached: 13 men with the pack train. Casualties on Last Stand Hill: 46 KIA.

Co. E: 1/Lt. Algernon E. Smith, 2/Lt. James G. Sturgis, plus 49 men. Detached: 11 men of whom 9 were with the pack train. -2 stragglers. Casualties on Last Stand Hill: 38 KIA.

Co. F: Capt. George W.M. Yates, 2/Lt. William Van Wyck Reily, plus 48 men. Detached: 11 men of whom 10 were with the pack train. -1 straggler. Casualties on Last Stand Hill: 38 KIA.

Reno's battalion

HQ: Maj. Marcus A. Reno commanding, plus three adjutants, two surgeons, one trumpeter, and seven men, plus two Quartermaster Department Interpreters, three Quartermaster Department scouts, 21 Arikara, four Dakota, and two Crows = 46 of all personnel. Casualties = 5 KIA and 2 WIA. Plus five company-grade officers and 144 men, of whom 1 officer and 24 men were on detached duty = 149. Casualties: 40 KIA and 25 WIA.

Co. A: Capt. Miles Moylan, 1/Lt. Charles C. DeRudio, plus 47 men. Detached: 8 men of whom 7 were with the pack train. Casualties: 8 KIA, 6 WIA = 14.

Co. G: 1/Lt. Donald McIntosh, 2/Lt. George Wallace, plus 43 men. Detached: 8 men of whom 7 were with the pack train. Casualties: 14 KIA, 5 WIA = 19.

Co. M: Capt. Thomas H. French, 1/Lt. Edward G. Mathey, plus 54 men. Detached: 8 men, plus 1/Lt. Mathey, with the pack train. Casualties: 12 KIA, 10 WIA = 22.

Benteen's battalion

HQ: Capt. Frederick W. Benteen, plus 1 Arikara scout, 5 company-grade officers, and 136 men, of whom 26 were on detached duty = 143 of all personnel. Casualties: 10 KIA, 23 WIA.

Co. H: 1/Lt. Francis M. Gibson, plus 45 men. Detached: 8 men of whom 7 were with the pack train. Casualties: 3 KIA, 17 WIA = 20.

Co. D: Capt. Thomas B. Weir, 2/Lt. Winfield S. Edgerly, plus 50 men. Detached: 7 men with the pack train. Casualties: 3 KIA, 3 WIA = 6.

Co. K: 1/Lt. Edward S. Godfrey, 2/Lt. Luther R. Hare, plus 41 men. Detached: 1 officer and 10 men of whom 6 were with the pack train. Casualties: 5 KIA, 3 WIA = 8.

Pack Train

Co. B: Capt. Thomas M. McDougall, 2/Lt. Benjamin H. Hodgson, plus 44 men = 46. Detached: 1 officer (Hodgson as Reno's adjutant) and 1 man. Casualties: 3 KIA, 4 WIA = 7.

Slim Buttes, September 9–10, 1876

Sioux and Cheyenne forces
American Horse plus Sioux and Cheyenne (44 lodges containing about 150 warriors).
Crazy Horse plus mixed band of *c.*700 warriors, including He Dog and Kicking Bear.

Crook's Column (Big Horn and Yellowstone Expedition)
Brig. Gen. George R. Crook commanding, plus one assistant adjutant general, three *aides-de-camp*, one acting commissary of subsistence, one medical director, two assistant surgeons, and five acting assistant surgeons = 14 of all personnel.

Cavalry Brigade (Col. Wesley Merritt, 5th Cavalry, plus two acting assistant adjutant generals and two *aides-de-camp*)

3d Cavalry Battalion (Maj. Andrew W. Evans, plus one adjutant): Co. A (1/Lt. Joseph Lawson, 2/Lt. Charles Morton); Co. B (Capt. Charles Meinhold, 2/Lt. James F. Simpson); Co. C (Capt. Frederick Van Vliet); Co. D (2/Lt. William W. Robinson, Jr); Co. E (1/Lt. Adolphus H. Von Luettwitz); Co. F (1/Lt. Alexander D.B. Smead, 2/Lt. Bainbridge Reynolds); Co. G (1/Lt. Emmet Crawford); Co. I (Capt. William H. Andrews, 1/Lt. Albert D. King, 2/Lt. James E.H. Foster); Co. L (Capt. Peter D. Vroom, 2/Lt. George F. Chase); Co. M (Capt. Anson Mills, 1/Lt. Augustus C. Paul, 2/Lt. Frederick G. Schwatka).

5th Cavalry (Lt. Col. Eugene A. Carr, plus one adjutant):
First Battalion (Maj. John J. Upham, plus one adjutant): Co. A (Capt. Calbraith P. Rodgers); Co. C (Capt. Emil Adam, 2/Lt. Edward L. Keyes); Co. G (Capt. Edward M.

Hayes); Co. I (Capt. Sanford C. Kellog, 1/Lt. Bernard Reilly, Jr., 2/Lt. Robert London, 2/Lt. Satterlee C. Plummer, 4th Infantry, attached); Co. M (Capt. Edward H. Leib).

Second Battalion (Maj. Julius W. Mason, plus one adjutant): Co. B (Capt. Robert H. Montgomery); Co. D (Capt. Samuel S. Sumner); Co. E (Capt. George F. Price); Co. F (Capt. John S. Payne, 1/Lt. Alfred B. Bache); Co. K (Capt. Albert E. Woodson).

2d Cavalry Battalion (Capt. Henry E. Noyes): Co. A (Capt. Thomas B. Dewees, 2/Lt. Daniel C. Pearson); Co. B (1/Lt. William C. Rawolle); Co. D (1/Lt. Samuel M. Swigert, 2/Lt. Henry D. Huntington); Co. E (Capt. Elijah R. Wells, 2/Lt. Frederick W. Sibley); Co. I (2/Lt. Frederick W. Kingsbury).

Infantry (Maj. Alexander Chambers): Co. D, 4th Infantry (1/Lt. Henry Seton); Co. F, 4th Infantry (Capt. Gerhard L. Luhn); Co. G, 4th Infantry (Capt. William H. Powell, 2/Lt. Albert B. Crittenden); Co. C, 9th Infantry (Capt. Samuel Munson, 1/Lt. Hayden D. Lany); Co. G, 9th Infantry (1/Lt. William L. Carpenter); Co. H, 9th Infantry (Capt. Andrew S. Burt, 2/Lt. Charles M. Rockefeller, 2/Lt. Edgar B. Robertson); Co. B, 14th Infantry (Capt. James Kennington, 1/Lt. John Murphy, 2/Lt. Charles F. Lloyd); Co. C, 14th Infantry (Capt. Daniel W. Burke); Co. F, 14th Infantry (Capt. Thomas F. Tobey, 2/Lt. Frederic S. Calhoun); Co. I, 14th Infantry (1/Lt. Frank Taylor, 2/Lt. Richard T. Yeatman).

Maj. W.S. Stanton, Engineers, commanding small irregular force.

Scouts (Capt. George M. Randall, 23d Infantry): Frank Grouard, William "Buffalo Bill" Cody, Baptiste "Big Bat" Pourier, Baptiste "Little Bat" Garnier, "Captain Jack" Crawford, Charles "Buffalo Chips" White.

SELECT BIBLIOGRAPHY

Bray, Kingsley M. (2006). *Crazy Horse: A Lakota Life*. Norman, OK: University of Oklahoma Press.

Brininstool, Earl Alonzo (1925). *A Trooper with Custer*. Columbus, OH: Hunter-Trade-Trapper Co.

Brininstool, Earl Alonzo (1933). *The Custer Fight. Capt. Benteen's Story of the Battle of the Little Big Horn, June 25–26, 1876*. Hollywood, CA: privately published.

Charger, Samuel (1928). "A Chronology of the Sioux from an Earlier Period," in *Sunshine Magazine*, Vol. 9, No. 8, December 1928: 304–315.

Finerty, John F. (1890). *Warpath and Bivouac or the Conquest of the Sioux*. Chicago, IL: Donohue & Henneberry.

Garland, Hamlin (1898). "General Custer's Last Fight as seen by Two Moons," in *McClure's Magazine*, Vol. 11, No. 5 (September): 443–448.

Godfrey, Edward S. (1892). "Custer's Last Battle. By One of his Troop Commanders," in *The Century Magazine*, January 1892: 358–384.

Graham, Lt. Col. W.A. (1923). "'Come on! Be Quick! Bring Packs!' Custer's Battle Plan: The Story of His Last Message, as Told by the Man Who Carried It," in *The Cavalry Journal*, Vol. 32 (July): 303–317.

Graham, W.A. (1986). *The Custer Myth: A Source Book of Custeriana*. Lincoln, NE: University of Nebraska Press.

Hardoff, Richard G. (2002). *On the Little Bighorn with Walter Camp 1865–1925: A Collection of W.M. Camp's Letters, Notes and Opinions on Custer's Last Fight*. El Segundo, CA: Upton & Sons.

Kanipe, Daniel A. (1903). "A New Story of Custer's Last Battle," in *Contributions to the Montana Historical Society*, Vol. IV: 277–283.

King, Captain Charles (1890). *Campaigning with Crook and Stories of Army Life*. New York, NY: Harper & Bros.

Lehman, Tim (2010). *Bloodshed at Little Bighorn: Sitting Bull, Custer, and the Destinies of Nations*. Baltimore, MD: Johns Hopkins University Press.

Libby, Orin Grant, ed. (1998). *The Arikara Narrative of Custer's Campaign and the Battle of the Little Bighorn*. Norman, OK: University of Oklahoma Press.

Mallery, Garrick (1893). "Picture Writing of the American Indians," 10th Annual Report of the Bureau of American Ethnology. Washington, DC: Government Printing Office: pp. 551–570.

Marquis, Thomas B. (1931). *A Warrior Who Fought*

Custer. Minneapolis, MN: The Midwest Co.
Morrison, Paul, ed. (2010). *Custer's Conqueror by William J. Bordeaux.* Bloomington, IN: Xlibris Corporation.
Schmidt, Martin F., ed. (1946). *General George Crook: his autobiography.* Norman, OK: University of Oklahoma Press.
Vaughn, J.W. (1956). *With Crook at the Rosebud.* Harrisburg, PA: Stackpole Co.
Vestal, Stanley (1934). *Warpath: The True Story of the Fighting Sioux Told in a Biography of Chief Joseph White Bull.* Boston, MA: Houghton Mifflin.
Wagner, Frederic C., III (2014). *The Strategy of Defeat at the Little Big Horn*: A Military and Timing Analysis of the Battle. Jefferson, NC: McFarland & Co.
Wagner, Frederic C., III (2016). *Participants in the Battle of the Little Big Horn.* 2d edition. Jefferson, NC: McFarland & Co.

Primary sources

Col. W.H. Wood to Assistant Adjutant General, Department of Dakota, February 27, 1877, Sioux War Papers, National Archives, Record Group 94 (Records of the Adjutant General's Office), Microfilm M666, Roll 280.

Crook-Kennon Papers, US Army Military History Institute, Carlisle Barracks, PA.

Edward Curtis Papers, "Thunder Bear's Version of Custer's Fight," General Collection #1143, Box 3, Folder 3.8, Natural History Museum of Los Angeles County, CA.

George Bird Grinnell Collection, Notebook 348, Braun Research Library, Southwest Museum, Los Angeles, CA.

Little Soldier interview by Joseph G. Masters, Box 2, Folder 15, Kansas State Historical Society, Topeka, KS (KSHS interview).

Lt. Col. George P. Buell to the Assistant Adjutant General, Department of Dakota, September 19, 1876, National Archives, Record Group 393 (Records of United States Army Continental Commands, 1823–1920), Item 7215.

Official Record of a Court of Inquiry convened at Chicago, Illinois, January 13, 1879, by the President of the United States upon the request of Major Marcus A. Reno, 7th US Cavalry, to investigate his conduct at the Battle of the Little Big Horn, June 25-26, 1876.

Philip Henry Sheridan papers, Library of Congress.

Records of United States Regular Army Mobile Units, 1821–1942. Record Group 391. Records of the 7th–10th Cavalry Regiments. Field Return of Seventh Cavalry, June 1876.

United States Statutes at Large (1866). 39th Congress, 1st Session. Washington, DC: Little, Brown & Co., 333.

US National Archives, M233, Army Register of Enlistments, 1798–1914: Registers of Enlistments 1871–1877.

Walter Camp Interview Notes, Box 4, Walter Mason Camp Collection, Archives and Manuscripts, Harold B. Lee Library, Brigham Young University, Provo, UT.

Newspapers

Army and Navy Journal, NY (*ANJ*); *Asheville Citizen Times*, Asheville, NC (*ACT*); *Atlanta Constitution and Journal*, GA (*AG&J*); *Chicago Tribune*, IL (*CT*); *Cincinnati Daily Enquirer*, OH (*CDE*); *Cleveland Leader*, OH (*CL*); *Daily Graphic*, NY (*DG*); *Daily Inter Ocean*, IL (*DIO*); *Daily Picuyune*, LA (*DP*); *Evening Star*, DC (*ES*); *Hardin Tribune*, MT (*HT*); *Helena Independent Record*, MT (*HIR*); *Jamestown Weekly Alert*, NC (*JWA*); *Leavenworth Times*, KS (*LT*); *Leavenworth Weekly Times*, KS (*LWT*); *New York Herald*, NY (*NYH*); *Northwestern Christian Advocate*, Chicago, IL (*NCA*); *Philadelphia Inquirer*, PA (*PI*); *San Francisco Chronicle*, CA (*SFC*).

INDEX

References to illustrations are shown in **bold**.

Andrews, Capt. William H. 28, **29**, 33, **63**
Arapaho 4, **50–51**, 52
Arikara scouts 42, 43, 56: Bloody Knife **56**
Assiniboine Sioux 7, 46
axes/tomahawks **46**, **50–51**, 52

Benteen, Capt. Frederick W. 25, 40, **41**, 42, 45, 46, 48, 52, 53, **53**, 55, 72
bow-lances/lances **10**, **11**, 16, 20, **50–51**, 52
bows and arrows 8, 20, **50–51**, 52, 54
Boyer, Michel "Mitch" 36, **38**, 42, 72

Calhoun, 1/Lt. James "Jimmi" **44**, 46
carbines 15, **15**, 18, 19, 21, **22**, 31, **50–51**, 52; **66–67**, 68
Carr, Lt. Col. Eugene A. **61**, **66–67**, 68
cavalry regts 12, 13, 21, 22
  2d 18, 31, 60, **61**, 65: bns 64; cos 23, 24, 25, 57: A 28, **29**; B/D/E/I 28, **29**, 31
  3d 18, **59**, **61**, 65: bns 64; cos 23, 25, 34, 57, 62: B 28, **29**, 33; C 28, **29**, 31, 33; D **14**, **15**, 28, **29**, 31; E 31, **61**, 62; F 28, **29**, 31; G 28, **29**, 31, 33, **61**, 62; I 28, **29**, 31, 33; M **26**, **61**, 62, 69
  4th 23
  5th 6, 18, 31, **61**, 64, 65, **66–67**, 68: cos 57: F **66–67**, 68; K 17, **66–67**, 68, 69
  7th 4, 6, 12, 13, 18, 19, 25, 37–38, 39, 40, **41**, 42, 43, 47, 56, 66, 71, 72: bns 38, 72; cos 25, 38: A 19, 42, 43, 45, 52, 53; B 19, **39**, 42, 48, 52; C 18, 19, 40, 42, 45, 46, 47, 56; D 19, 40, 42, 52; E 18, 19, 42, 46, 48, 52; F 19, 42, 46, 48; G 19, 42, 43, 52, 53; H 19, 42, 45, 48, 52, 53, 54; I 19, 40, 42, 46, 73, 74; K 13, 17, 19, 42, 52, 53; L 13, 18, 19, 31, 40, 42, 44, 46, 54; M 13, 18, 19, 42, 43–44, 52, 53, 54
Chambers, Maj. Alexander 27, 28, **29**, 31, 33, **61**
Cheyenne chiefs 46: Two Moons 4, 44, 46, 55–56; White Bird 55
Cheyenne scouts 30, 35
Cheyenne warriors 4, 5, 6, 17, 21, 28, **29**, 30, 31–32, 34, 38, 39, 40, 48, **50–51**, 52, 55–56, 70, 71, 73: Wooden Leg 30, 31, 32; Young Two Moon 34, 72
clubs/war clubs **50–51**, 52
Cooke, 1/Lt. William W. 40, 42, 43, 45–46, 48, **50–51**, 52
couriers/messengers 31, 33, 34, 36, 40, 45, 47, 48, **48**, 60, 64
Crawford, 1/Lt. Emmett **61**, 62
Crook, Brig. Gen. George R. 6, 7, 10, 16, 17, 20, 23–24, 25–26, **25**, 26–27, **26**, 27, 28, **29**, 30, 31, **31**, 32, 33, 34–35, **34**, 36, 37, 57, 58, 60, **61**, 62, 64, 65, 66, 69, 70, 71, 73
Crow chiefs: Feather Head/Good Heart/Old Crow/Medicine Crow 27
Crow scouts/warriors 25, 27, 28, **29**, 30, 31, **32**, 33, 34, **35**, 38, 39, 42, 72, **72**, 75: Curly 72, 75; Goes Ahead 72; Hairy Moccasin 71; Half Yellow Face 72; White Man Runs Him 71
Custer, Capt. Tom 18, 45, 49, **50–51**, 52, 54
Custer, Lt. Col. George A. 5, 6, **13**, 18, **18**, 46: at Little Bighorn 4, 6, 7, 18, 19, 24–25, 36, 37, 38, 39, 40, **41**, 42, 44, 45–46, 47, 48, 49, **50–51**, 52, 53, 55, 56, 66, 71–72; death of 5, 40, 49, **49**, **50–51**, 52, 55, 56, 71, **72**, 75

Dakota Territory 4–5, 6, 7, 23, 46, 47, 58, 60
District of Montana 6, 23, 24

Evans, Maj. Andrew W. 28, **29**, 31, **61**

forts 4: Abraham Lincoln 6, 7, **12**, **13**, 23, 24, 48, 74; Benton 7; Buford 7, 46; C.F. Smith 7; DuChesne 53; Ellis 7, 24; F.D. Pease 7, 24; Fetterman 6, 7, 23, 25, 36; Laramie 6, 7, 34; Leavenworth 72; Meade 72; Peck 7; Phil Kearny 7, 25; Randall 7; Reno 23, 25; Shaw 6, 7, 23, 24; Totten 7, 47; Yates 46

Gibbon, Col. John 6, 7, 23, 24, **24**, 25, 36, 37, 38
Godfrey, 1/Lt. Edward S. 17, **41**, 52, 53
Grouard, Frank 23, 25, 27, 28, 34, **34**, 60, 62, **63**, 64

Henry, Capt. Guy V. 27, 28, **29**, 31, 32, 33, 34
Herendeen, George 9, 38, 39, 42, 43, 44, 54
Hunkpapa Sioux: Crow King **9**, 42–43, 44, 49, 54, 55

Indian agencies/reservations 4, 5–6, 7, 17, 46, 57, 62, 64, 74, 75
infantry regts 21, 23, 27, 30, 31, 32, 33, 34, 36, 57, 60, 62
  4th 28, **29**: cos 25, 57, 65: D/F 28, **29**; G 64; I 62
  6th 25
  7th 57: cos 24
  9th 28, **29**, 60, **61**: cos 23, 25, 57, 65: C 28, **29**; G/H 31, 33
  14th **61**: cos 57, 65
  17th 57: cos 25
  20th 24
  22d 57
  23d 31, 33
interpreters 25, 34, 36, **38**, 64, 72

Kanipe, Sgt. Daniel A. 18, 40, 45, 47, **47**, 48
Keogh, Capt. Myles W. 18, 40, **41**, 44, 46, 47, 48, 73, 74
King, 1/Lt. Charles 17, 31, 68, 69
knife clubs **66–67**, 68
knives **10**, 11, **50–51**, 52

Lakota Sioux 4, 5: American Horse 6, 60, 62, 64, 65, **66–67**, 68, 73; Charging Bear **65**; Crazy Horse 4, 5, 6, 9, 21, 23, 27, 30, 40, 47, **50–51**, 52, 56, 69, **66–67**, 68, 73, 74
Little Bighorn (the), battle of 4, 6, 9, 13, 17, 18–19, 36–40, **41**, 42–49, **44**, 45, 48, 49, **50–51**, 52, 52–56, 54, 55, 56, 66, 71–72, 74, 75, 75: "Battle Ridge" **41**, 47; "Calhoun Hill" 9, 40, **41**, 44, 46–47; "Cemetery Ridge" 40, **41**, 47, 48; "Crow's Nest" 38, 39; "Last Stand Hill" 4, 5, 6, 18, 40, **41**, 47, 48, **50–51**, 52, 52, 54, 55, 72; "Reno Hill" 40, **41**; "Weir Point" **41**, 52–53; order of battle 76–77
Luettwitz, 1/Lt. Adolphus H. Von **61**, 62

McDougall, Capt. Thomas M. 39, 40, **41**, 45, 47, 52
Meinhold, Capt. Charles 28, **29**, 33
Mills, Capt. Anson 6, 26, 27, 28, **29**, 31, 33, 34, 60, **61**, 62–63, **63**, 64, 66
Miniconjou Sioux chiefs: Lame Deer 75; Red Horse 44–45, 49, 58, 63, 64, 69
Montana Territory 4, 6, 7, 18, 24, 74, 75

Nihil, Pvt. "Paddy" **66–67**, 68
Northern Cheyenne chiefs 4, 32
Northern Cheyenne warriors: Buffalo-Calf-Road-Woman 32, 49, **50–51**, 52; Tall Bull **65**
Noyes, Capt. Henry E. 27, 28, **29**, 33, 34, **61**

Oglala Sioux 46, **46**

Packers and Miners 28, **29**, 33, 49, 56, 62

Reno, Maj. Marcus A. 6, 18–19, 25, 36–37, 38, 40, **41**, 42, 43–45, **43**, 45, 46, 47, 48, 49, 52, 52–55, 56, 72, 77
repeating rifles 17, **66–67**, 68
revolvers **13**, **14**, 15, 17, 18, 31, **50–51**, 52, **66–67**, 68
Reynolds, "Lonesome" Charley **38**, 43
Rosebud (the), battle of 6, **10**, **11**, **14**, **15**, **16**, 17, 21, 22–28, **25**, **26**, **27**, 28, **29**, 30–35, **32**, **35**, **36**, 37, 38, 42, 57–58, 70–71: order of battle 76
Royall, Lt. Col. William B. **14**, **16**, 27, 28, **29**, 31, 32, 33, 34, **63**, 70

Sans Arc Sioux 42, 58: Many Shields **58**, 64
Schreiber, Sgt. Lucifer **66–67**, 68
Schwatka, 2/Lt. Frederick G. 60, **61**, 62, **63**
scouts/scouting 4, 9, 34, **34**, 36, 38, **38**, 39, 42, 43, 44, 45, 54, 60, 62, **63**, 64, 69, 71, 72: Native Americans 20, 23, 25, 27, **29**, 30, **32**, 33, 34, **35**, 35, 37, 38, **38**, 42, 43, 56, **56**, 57, 58, **72**, 73, 75
Sheridan, Lt. Gen. Philip H. 6, 7, 23, **23**, 58
Shoshone allies/scouts 25, **26**, 27, 28, **29**, 30, 31, 32, **32**, 33, 34, 73
Sioux chiefs 55: He Dog **66–67**, 68; Iron Thunder **66–67**, 68; Kicking Bear **66–67**, 68; Low Dog **44**, 46, **46**, 49; Red Cloud 5; Sitting Bull 5, 6, 25, 34, **37**, 38, 44, 46, 47–48, 57, 72, 74, 75; Spotted Tail 5
Sioux scouts 20, 27, 35
Sioux warriors 7, **10**, **10**, **11**, 30, 31, 34, 39, 57, 73
  battle-honor system **11**, **11**, 16, 20–21, **46**, **50–51**, 52, 54–55, **66–67**, 68
  clothing **10**, 11, **11**, 20–21, **46**, **50–51**, 52, **66–67**, 68
  fighting prowess/tactics 4, 5, 6, 8, **16**, 20, 21, 23, **24**, 26, 28, **29**, 30, 31–32, 33, 34, 35, **35**, 38, 40, **41**, 43–45, 46, 47, 48, 49, **50–51**, 52, 53, 54, 55–56, 65, **66–67**, 68, 70, 71, 72, 75
  footwear **11**, **11**, **50–51**, 52
  headgear 16: trailer war bonnets **16**, **16**, **26**, **50–51**, 52, **66–67**, 68
Sioux warriors (individuals): Gall **50–51**, 52, 53; Hump **49**; Lazy White Bull **10**, 35; Little Buck Elk 52; Little Hawk 27, 32; Little Soldier 44; Lone Horn 4; Thunder Bear **45**
Slim Buttes, battle of 57–58, **59**, 60, **61**, 62–65, **66–67**, 68, 69, **73**, 73: order of battle 77–78

Terry, Brig. Gen. Alfred H. 6, 7, 13, 23, 24–25, **25**, 36, 37, 38, 55, 57, 58, 70, 71, 72, 75

US cavalry forces
  clothing/uniforms **14**, **15**, 15, 17–18, **22**, 31, **47**, 53, **66–67**, 68, 73: rank insignia/stripes **14**, **15**, 17, **18**, 48
  footwear **14**, 15, 17, 31, **66–67**, 68
  formations/tactics 21–22, **22**, 31: skirmish lines/skirmishers 21–22, 26, 28, **29**, 31, 33, 40, **41**, 43, 62, 65, **66–67**, 68
  headgear **14**, **15**, 17, 18, **22**, 31, **31**, **66–67**, 68
  recruitment and training 12–13, 17

Van Vliet, Capt. Frederick 27, 28, **29**, 31, 33, **59**
Van Wyck Reily, 2/Lt. William **50–51**, 52
Varnum, 2/Lt. Charles A. 25, 38, 39, 42

warrior societies 8, 16, 55
war shields **11**, **11**, **50–51**, **66–67**, 68
Weir, Capt. Thomas B. 40, **41**, 52, 53
Wyoming Territory 4, 6, 7, 23